A Naturalist's (

MAMMALS OF
SOUTHEAST ASIA

Brunei, Cambodia, Indonesia, Laos,
Malaysia, Myanmar, the Philippines,
Singapore, Thailand and Vietnam

Chris R. Shepherd and Loretta Ann Shepherd

Consultant: Will Duckworth

JOHN BEAUFOY PUBLISHING

First published in the United Kingdom in 2012 by John Beaufoy Publishing
11 Blenheim Court, 316 Woodstock Road, Oxford OX2 7NS, England
www.johnbeaufoy.com

10 9 8 7 6 5 4 3 2

ISBN 978-1-906780-71-5

Photo captions
Front cover: *top left* Tiger (Stephen Hogg/Wildtrack Photography); *top right* Asian Elephant (James Eaton/
Birdtour Asia); *bottom left* Cream-coloured Giant Squirrel (Nick Baker, EcologyAsia.com); *bottom middle*
Sumatran Rhinoceros (Stephen Hogg/Wildtrack Photography); *bottom right* Long-tailed Macaque (Chris
R. Shepherd). **Back cover:** Common Palm Civet (Chris R. Shepherd). **Title page:** Fishing Cat (Abraham
Matthew/Singapore Zoo and Night Safari). **Contents page:** Siamang (Vilma D'Rozario/Cicada Tree Eco-Place).

Illustrations by Stephen Dew

Dedication
For our daughter Raven Dhanya Shepherd.

Edited and designed by D & N Publishing, Baydon, Wiltshire, UK

Printed and bound in Malaysia by Times Offset (M) Sdn. Bhd.

·CONTENTS·

Introduction

Globally, there are over 5,500 species of mammals. More than 800 occur naturally in South-East Asia, and many of these are found nowhere else in the world. An increasing number of South-East Asia's mammals are severely threatened – directly by hunting and the wildlife trade, and indirectly by habitat loss, urbanisation, the introduction of non-native species, etc. Conservation actions for the region's mammals have never been so urgently needed.

Despite the region boasting such an amazing wealth of species, and despite many of these slipping precariously close to the edge of extinction, most people have very limited knowledge, awareness or appreciation of these animals or their needs. Fewer still realise that each of us can play a role in ensuring that this incredibly varied yet intertwined myriad of species remains intact for generations to come.

This book is intended to play a part in just that – raising awareness and interest in the region's mammals, and encouraging more people to get involved in protecting these species and their fragile habitats. We sincerely hope that you enjoy the photographs featured here and find the information useful. We hope that with this guide you will have a greater appreciation for South-East Asia's wildlife, and that you will be inspired to play your part, be it by becoming a more responsible citizen, by reducing your impact on the environment around you, by pledging to support individuals or organisations working to better understand and protect mammals and other wildlife, or by choosing to become directly involved in research and conservation yourself.

South-East Asia here refers to the countries of Brunei, Cambodia, Indonesia (Greater Sundas only – Java, Borneo, Sumatra and associated smaller islands, with the line being drawn immediately east of Bali), Laos, Malaysia, Myanmar, the Philippines, Singapore, Thailand and Vietnam. This area is home to a vast variety of mammals living in an amazingly wide range of habitats, from mountaintops to the sea, brackish mangroves and vast wetlands, to tall rainforests, dry open forests and rugged limestone hills. Increasingly,

secondary forest habitats are home to many species and are therefore worthy of conservation efforts as well. Some more adaptable species are even found in plantations and agricultural areas, and living alongside humans in rural and occasionally even urban settings – though it is important to recognise that the more habitat is lost, the more the variety and viability of the mammal communities living within suffers.

Riverine species, such as the Proboscis Monkey (*Nasalis larvatus*), can be viewed fairly easily on the Kinabatangan river in Sabah, Malaysia.

USING THIS BOOK

This book is not intended to be a comprehensive field guide, instead aiming to introduce readers to a selection of the 800 species of mammals native to South-East Asia. There are 129 species accounts featured in these pages, with photographs and notes on each, including a basic description, information on the species' range and preferred habitats, and a variety of other interesting points.

The majority of the images we have used are of wild mammals, photographed in their natural state, but a few are of captive individuals, largely because of the rarity of the species in question, or because of the unavailability of suitable wild images showing the identification features. A number are remote camera-trap images taken by researchers. These camera traps, as they are usually referred to, have become essential tools in the field of mammal research and conservation. With such devices positioned in the forest, invaluable photographs and information can be collected – anything from basic presence or absence to far more detailed data, such as aiding in identifying individual Tigers (*Panthera tigris*) by their unique stripe patterns. Camera traps can remain far longer in the field than a researcher, and are much less disruptive to the wildlife. We have deliberately included a few pictures taken with camera traps, although the picture quality is sometimes lower than that of a photo taken in captivity, to give the reader a sense of the research being carried out.

A brief description of the main features of each species is given, to assist in identification. Standard measurements are given as follows (see also diagrams below):

HB   head and body
T   tail length
TL   total length (for cetaceans and sirenians)

SH   shoulder height (for larger mammals)
FA   forearm (for bats)

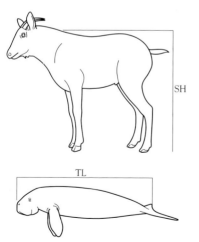

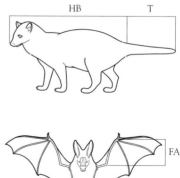

Measurements refer to adult animals. It is important to remember that sizes may vary greatly, and in some cases there is great variety in both size and colour within a single species.

A brief description of the known habitat, or habitats, used by each species is also given. A few notes are also provided on the habits or ecology of the species. It is important to remember that habitat use of many species may vary, sometimes seasonally, sometimes due to the loss of preferred habitat. Others are generalists and use a wide variety of habitats or are able to adapt not only to a number of natural settings but also to alterations made by humans. Some species can adapt to extreme habitat alteration, while others leave or simply perish once their habitat has been disturbed. Loss of habitat is one of the greatest threats to South-East Asia's mammals.

We have included a checklist of the mammals found in the region, which we have attempted to make as complete and accurate as possible, based on available information – though we acknowledge that there may be omissions. We hope this checklist forms the basis for future additions, as new mammals are being discovered all the time. We have relied heavily on the IUCN Red List of Threatened Species, and various regional field guides and country species lists (see Further Information), especially *A Field Guide to the Mammals of South-East Asia* by Charles M. Francis. Introduced species, and species already considered extinct, such as Schomburgk's Deer (*Rucervus schomburgki*), are not included in this list. Others, such as the Kouprey (*Bos sauveli*), which is likely to be extinct, and the Sika (*Rucervus nippon*), which is likely to be extirpated from South-East Asia, are still included in the checklist, in the countries they were originally found in, as they have not yet been officially declared extinct or extirpated.

Included also is the current status of each species according to the IUCN Red List. As the status of species is periodically revised, readers should check the current status at www.iucnredlist.org.

WHAT'S IN A NAME?

All species have a scientific (usually 'Latinised') name. This nomenclature is to avoid confusion, as common names vary in different languages and locations, but the scientific binomial (two-part) names are used universally. The first part of the scientific name – *Panthera*, for example – denotes the genus, the second part – e.g. *tigris* – the species within that genus: *Panthera tigris*, the Tiger. A third name is added when referring to a subspecies: *Panthera tigris sumatrae*, the Sumatran Tiger.

Common names used, in English, are also given in this book, to make it convenient for people unfamiliar with scientific names. However, common names can be confusing, as there is often more than one for a single species (for example, Silvered Langur, Silvered Leaf Monkey, Silvered Monkey, Silvery Lutung are all names for *Trachypithecus cristatus*). In an attempt to standardise the common names in the region, where possible we have used the same names as Charles M. Francis in *A Field Guide to the Mammals of South-East Asia*. As this is the most recent and comprehensive guide for the mainland of South-East Asia, it makes little sense to vary the names yet again and further confuse the issue. For example, we have taken the lead from Francis and eliminated the terms leaf monkey, surili and lutung, instead calling them all langurs. Having said that, some of the names in this book do differ or are slightly modified, based on recommendations from Duckworth and Pine's 2003 paper on 'English names for a world list of mammals' (see Further Information). Furthermore, the geographic coverage in Francis's book does not include Brunei, Indonesia, Malaysian Borneo (Sabah and Sarawak), the Philippines and Singapore, and therefore names were obtained elsewhere for species occurring in these countries.

The taxonomy of the region's mammals is far from being finalised, and much more work in this field is urgently needed. Many of the species are likely in fact to represent complexes of more than one species. What now appears to be a single widespread and common species may actually include a number of localised and threatened species that require urgent conservation assistance.

OPPORTUNITIES FOR NATURALISTS

While South-East Asia is one of the wealthiest regions in the world in terms of species diversity, very little is actually known about the ecology, habits, status, threats and conservation needs of the majority of its mammals. It is hoped that with more people – biologists, naturalists, local inhabitants and visitors from overseas – observing and learning about mammals in their natural habitat, the result will be that these information gaps are filled.

Montane forests are important habitats for a variety of species throughout the region.

MAMMAL WATCHING

While many amazing mammals occur here, finding them is the trick. In some parts of the region, some are quite easy to find, especially diurnal mammals that can live in close proximity to people (in areas where people are not hunting them), such as some monkeys and squirrels. But the vast majority of them are more challenging. Some mammal species have only been seen a few times ever!

Some simple tools are a good pair of binoculars, identification guides and a notebook – and a torch or headlamp to find nocturnal mammals. A healthy dose of patience is also useful. Finding mammals is not always easy, and once they have been detected, they often flee. Many are nocturnal and/or arboreal, further adding to the list of challenges. It is important to follow some basic principles of keeping noise levels low, wearing mute-coloured field clothes, moving quietly and cautiously, and paying attention to animal sounds and signs. The call of gibbons, for instance, may reveal a dueting pair, marks on trees may be clues to the presence of bears, and busy footprints may lead to a herd of deer.

Identifying mammals – especially small mammals, where clear views are not always possible because they are hidden or are fleeing, and which in many cases closely resemble other species – takes some practice. Do not be discouraged. Take notes on what you have seen, including description, location, habitat, altitude, behaviour, and other details of the encounter. This will help confirm the identity of the mystery mammal, and could very likely contribute to the current pool of knowledge.

Very little is known about most of the mammals of South-East Asia. Increased knowledge, whether through basic field observations or from intense research, is desperately needed in order better to understand the needs of each and ultimately to try and prevent the loss of any more species from the wild. Acquiring suitable photographs for this book was challenging, highlighting the need for more photographers, amateur and professional, to get out there and take pictures, especially of the more secretive and little-known species. There is not a great deal of information on most of the region's mammals, so every observation, record and photograph taken is potentially an important contribution to the overall understanding of that species' behaviour, ecology and requirements.

WILDLIFE IN TROUBLE

Sadly, an increasing number of South-East Asia's mammals are threatened. At the time of writing this book more than 190 are considered Threatened (94 Vulnerable, 75 Endangered, 21 Critically Endangered) in the IUCN Red List, the most comprehensive evaluation of the conservation status of the world's plant and animal species (www.iucnredlist.org). Human-related activities are directly or indirectly responsible for the threatened status, and more species are being added to the list all the time.

HABITAT LOSS

Habitat loss and fragmentation is a serious threat to the conservation of most mammals in South-East Asia. Development – residential and agricultural expansion, especially for

Habitat loss: a severe threat to many of the region's mammals.

oil palm – has replaced large areas of habitat crucial to many mammal species. Highways and roads cut through forests, not only reducing the available space and limiting the movements of many species, but also increasing access for hunters. Logging activities degrade and destroy pristine habitat. While a few mammal species can survive in these disturbed habitats, and a few more at the edges, most cannot. Large-scale monoculture plantations in particular are a major threat to the continued survival of many species, destroying habitats, isolating populations, and bringing some species, such as Tigers, Leopards (*Panthera pardus*), Asian Elephants (*Elephas maximus*), Asian Black Bears (*Ursus thibetanus*) and Eurasian Wild Pigs (*Sus scrofa*), into conflict with people. In almost all such conflicts, the wildlife is the loser.

Steps must be taken to minimise the negative impact of development. Key habitats and connecting corridors must be set aside. Forests along rivers and other water bodies should be left intact, to maintain habitat and to allow wildlife access to water. Long-term land-use planning, be it for plantations, roads, farming or other development, must take the conservation of wildlife and wild places into consideration. In South-East Asia, where human population growth and expansion is taking place at a frightening pace, this is a major challenge. But not impossible.

TRADE IN WILDLIFE

Illegal and unsustainable trade, both domestic and international, is a growing threat to a rapidly increasing number of species, and nowhere is this more obvious and urgent than in South-East Asia. Wildlife has been harvested and traded throughout this region for thousands of years, yet never have the levels of harvesting and trade been as intense and as destructive as has been observed over the past few decades. Amongst all the threats wildlife faces, illegal trade is an extremely urgent issue that needs the highest level of attention, as it has the greatest potential to do maximum harm in a short time.

Humans have always exploited wildlife. Since the early times, our ancestors relied on meat from wild animals, and used their skins for clothing and shelter. As early as 2600 BC, rhinoceros horn and other animal parts were used in medicines. Emperors and other rulers kept elephants, to be used in war and ceremonies, and elephant ivory has been traded for centuries. There are records, for example, of Thailand exporting ivory to China and Japan dating back several centuries. In the 13th century, Thailand exported tusks to Fukien Province, China, and in the 19th century there is a record of Thailand exporting 18 tonnes of tusks to China.

Today, many of South-East Asia's mammals are severely threatened by trade – and in many cases this poses a greater threat than habitat loss. Civets are kept in cramped cages, fed coffee beans for the civet coffee or coffee luwak industry. Primates are eaten, as well as being traded for biomedical research and the pet industry. Cats are traded for their bones, meat and skins, while bears are hunted for their paws and gallbladders, or captured and kept in bear bile extraction facilities.

Many of these species, like the elephants killed to supply ivory demand centuries ago, are hunted to satisfy the demand from East Asia, especially China. Tigers and rhinos are prime examples, with their bones and horns, respectively, being highly prized in traditional Asian medicine. This demand has caused these species to become all but extinct in the wild. Suitable habitat for both Tigers and rhinos still remains in many places, but the animals are gone.

More resources and efforts must be channelled towards preventing any more species being lost to these threats. It is, however, not too late. We hope this book will encourage you to do what you can to support the conservation of South-East Asia's mammals.

GLOSSARY

agouti – coat colour type that has banding or stripes on individual hairs

allomothering – non-maternal care of infants

anthropogenic – caused by humans

antlers – bony, branched structures protruding from the front of the skull, shed annually, unlike horns, which are not branched and are permanent

arboreal – tree-dwelling

axillary – near the armpit region

beak – dolphin's snout

bovid – member of the Bovidae (cattle) family

brachiate – to move by swinging on the arms from one handhold to another

cephalopod – marine molluscs such as cuttlefish, squid and octopus

cetacean – whales, dolphins and porpoises

colobine – member of the Colobinae subfamily of primates

commensal – two species living in close association without harming each other

crepuscular – active at dawn and dusk

dew toes – hind toes that are a little smaller than the hoofs, which do not usually reach the ground except when there is soft soil

dipterocarp – tall, hardwood tropical tree species in the family Dipterocarpaceae that can grow to an exceptionally large size

distal – away from the body, towards the end

diurnal – active during the day

dorsal – the back surface or back part of the body

echolocation – determining the location

of an object by relying on echoes of sounds emitted

endemic – native species restricted to a particular geographic area

epiphytic – a plant that grows attached to another plant but does not cause the host any damage

falcate – sickle-shaped curve

family, genus and species – scientific classifications are used to categorise organisms into seven major divisions, which are known as taxa. The final three (family, genus and species) are the most specific of the categories, and show how closely related organisms are. For instance, members of the same genus are more closely related than members of the same family

fluke – each lobe of the tail of a cetacean or sirenian

frugivorous – having a diet mainly of fruit

fusiform – tapering at both ends

genus – *see* family, genus and species

horn – paired, bony, permanent growth on the upper part of the heads of certain hoofed mammals such as cattle, sheep and goats, usually curved or pointed; also similar pointed growth on the snout of rhinoceros

interfemoral membrane – the skin between the hind legs and tail of a bat, also known as the uropatagium

karst – rough and rocky landscape that comprises caves, underground channels and sinkholes, which is formed when the underground water dissolves soluble layers of bedrock such as limestone and dolomite

melanistic – high concentration of dark pigmentation that causes an overall appearance of dark colouration

melon – large and rounded forehead area of a dolphin

montane – mountainous area

morph – form or type within a species, usually referring to a colour variation with

no taxonomic significance

morphology – physical form and structure of an organism

nocturnal – active during the night

noseleaf (bats) – skin around the nose

pantropical – throughout the tropics

patagium – gliding membrane between fore and hind limbs, enclosing the tail

pedicel (deer) – bony base on forehead that supports the antlers

pelage – coat of a mammal (such as fur, wool, hair)

prehensile – tip (mainly of tail, snout, lips) that can curl and grasp objects

premaxilla – small bones at the tip of the jaw, supporting incisors

primary habitat/forest – old-growth forest that has never been logged

proboscis – long and flexible snout

sacculated – stomach with many chambers that aids digestion of high volumes of plant material

secondary habitat/forest – forest that has been logged but has recovered

species – *see* family, genus and species

split (taxonomy) – dividing further, to represent more than one group

subspecies – division within a species, distinct from other members of the same species, but not so distinct as to be considered a separate species

sub-montane – foothills of mountainous areas

sympatric – more than one species sharing the same geographic area

taxonomy – scientific system of classifying and identifying organisms

terrestrial – ground-dwelling

tine – prong on an antler

tusk (elephants, dugongs, etc.) – elongated, protruding tooth, usually in pairs

ventral – underside

vibrissae – long, stiff whisker hairs on snout and brows

Sunda Pangolin ■ *Manis javanica* HB 40–65cm, T 35–56cm

DESCRIPTION The entire upperparts, including the tail, are covered in brownish scales. It has very small ears, and a long and tapered head. Its underparts have no scales. It has very long claws.

DISTRIBUTION Brunei, Cambodia, Indonesia (Java, Kalimantan, Sumatra), Laos, Malaysia, Myanmar, Singapore, Thailand and Vietnam.

HABITS AND HABITAT Largely nocturnal, sleeping in an underground burrow during the day. Tall and secondary forest are the preferred habitat. Highly specialised diet of ants and termites, which it extracts using its strong claws and long sticky tongue from nests in trees, on and below the ground. The prehensile tail is especially useful when the pangolin is climbing trees.

NOTES When alarmed, it curls into a ball and wraps its tail around itself to protect its non-scaly underparts. It is heavily poached and traded for its purported medicinal properties, with populations declining severely throughout its range.

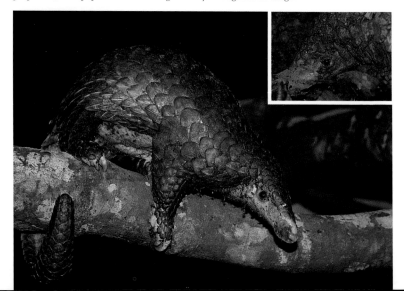

Chinese Pangolin ■ *Manis pentadactyla* HB 40–58cm, T 25–38cm

DESCRIPTION The upperparts, including the tail, are covered in brown scales, and it has more prominent ears than the Sunda Pangolin (p. 12). The scales on its head extend only part-way to the nostrils. It has long claws, which are longer on the forelimbs. Its tail is less flexible than the Sunda Pangolin's and considerably shorter, relative to the head-and-body length.

DISTRIBUTION Laos, Myanmar, Thailand and Vietnam. Also found in Bangladesh, Bhutan, China, Hong Kong, India, Nepal and Taiwan.

HABITS AND HABITAT The Chinese Pangolin is very similar to the Sunda Pangolin, also being nocturnal, living in tall primary and secondary forest and having a highly specialised diet of termites and ants.

NOTES This species has been seriously impacted by poaching and trade for its purported medicinal properties.

> **Moonrats and Gymnures**
> Moonrats and gymnures belong to the Erinaceidae family, which also includes
> hedgehogs, but they lack sharp spines.

Moonrat

■ *Echinosorex gymnura*
HB 32–40cm, T 20–29cm

DESCRIPTION In most of the
range the front part of the body
is white to greyish white and the remainder is black with greyish frosting. In Borneo, and
occasionally elsewhere, this large insectivore is all white with a sparse scattering of black
hairs. The tail is long and scaly, with short hair, dark at the base and light towards the end.
It has an elongated snout with a pinkish nose.

DISTRIBUTION Brunei, Indonesia (Kalimantan and Sumatra), Malaysia (Peninsular
Malaysia, Sabah and Sarawak), southernmost Myanmar and southernmost Thailand.

HABITS AND HABITAT Primary and secondary lowland forests, including mangroves
and swamp forests. Also found in hill forests. The species can also tolerate some habitat
disturbance. From sea level to 1,000m.

NOTES The moonrat has a strong pungent odour.

Short-tailed Gymnure

■ *Hylomys suillus* HB 12–14cm, T 2–3cm

DESCRIPTION Upperparts reddish brown to
dark brown, with a grey tinge. Underparts light
grey, with white-tipped hairs. Resembles a shrew,
with long snout, but has a very short hairless tail.

DISTRIBUTION Brunei, Cambodia, Indonesia
(Java, Kalimantan, Sumatra), Laos, Malaysia (Peninsular Malaysia, Sabah and Sarawak),
Myanmar, Thailand and Vietnam. Also found in China.

HABITS AND HABITAT Active day and night. In hill and montane forests up to 3,000m,
but sometimes in humid lowland forests. Feeds mainly on insects but also takes some fruit.

NOTES The life span of the Short-tailed Gymnure does not normally exceed 2 years.

> **TREESHREWS**
> Treeshrews are often confused with squirrels, with their similar body shape and tails, but they can be distinguished easily by their long pointed muzzles.

Mountain Treeshrew ■ *Tupaia montana* HB 15–22cm, T 13–19cm

DESCRIPTION The upperparts of this species vary from dark brown to reddish or olive-brown, always with fine reddish speckling. Its underparts are buffy red. Some individuals have a pale shoulder stripe. Very similar to the Common Treeshrew (p. 16), but has smaller hind feet and usually occurs at higher altitudes.

DISTRIBUTION Endemic to Borneo: Brunei, Indonesia (Kalimantan) and Malaysia (Sabah and Sarawak).

HABITS AND HABITAT Diurnal, though most active in early morning and late afternoon. Found only in sub-montane and montane primary and slightly disturbed secondary forests, usually above 600m. Largely terrestrial.

NOTES This is one of the most common, and easily observed, montane mammals in Sabah.

Common Treeshrew ■ *Tupaia glis* HB 13–21cm, T 12–20cm

DESCRIPTION Reddish-brown body with darker brownish-grey tail and head. Underside lighter to yellowish, often with a whitish stripe over the shoulder. Light eye-ring. Long pointed muzzle with sharp pointed teeth. It has short limbs and a long squirrel-like bushy tail.

DISTRIBUTION Indonesia (Java, Sumatra), Malaysia (Peninsular Malaysia), Singapore and Thailand.

HABITS AND HABITAT Diurnal. Mainly in lowland forests below 1,500m. Also in parks and plantations, and in some places, such as in Peninsular Malaysia, has adapted to suburban gardens. These small mammals feed on insects and fruit. Usually seen alone or in pairs, foraging on the ground or in low trees and bushes.

NOTES The name 'treeshrew' is misleading, as they are not shrews. Looking more like squirrels than shrews, the treeshrews have long been a family of confused identity – they were once even considered primates.

> **COLUGOS**
> Colugos are also known as flying lemurs, but this is an obvious misnomer as they glide rather than fly, and they aren't lemurs. They have a gliding membrane called the patagium between fore and hind limbs, enclosing the tail. There are a number of other mammals that glide from tree to tree, such as flying squirrels (pp. 126–130), but their feet and tail are free of the patagium.

Sunda Colugo ▪ *Galeopterus variegatus* HB 33–42cm, T 18–27cm

DESCRIPTION The Sunda Colugo is grey to reddish brown. The shaded and mottled coat camouflages the animal perfectly against tree bark.

DISTRIBUTION Brunei, Cambodia, Indonesia (Java, Kalimantan, Sumatra), Laos, Malaysia, Myanmar, Thailand, Singapore and Vietnam.

HABITS AND HABITAT Nocturnal but sometimes active during the day. Found in evergreen forest below 1,000m above sea level. Completely arboreal, clinging to the sides of trees and gliding between tall trees. Diet mainly leaves and flowers.

NOTES Females carry their young enclosed in the patagium. Some males have also been observed doing the same, though it is unlikely that they play a very large parenting role.

LEFT: *Adult.* RIGHT: *Juvenile*

Philippine Colugo ▪ *Cynocephalus volans* HB 33–38cm, T 17–27cm

DESCRIPTION Brown or grey-brown dorsal fur, with the males darker than the females. Has a patagium like the Sunda Colugo (p. 17).

DISTRIBUTION Philippines.

HABITS AND HABITAT Found in lowland primary, secondary and mixed forest and also disturbed habitat. Diet mainly leaves, rarely fruit. Nocturnal and crepuscular, completely arboreal, also clinging to the sides of trees and gliding between tall trees.

> **Bats**
> Bats are the only mammals that are able to truly fly.

Large Flying-fox ▪ *Pteropus vampyrus* HB 27–32cm, T absent, FA 18–20cm

DESCRIPTION Most fruit bats rely on sight and smell to find their way, which is why they have large, reflective eyes. The Large Flying-fox, the largest of the fruit bats, most likely has the greatest wingspan of any bat, reaching 1.5m. Fur colour is variable, but usually the body is black while the upper shoulders, the chest and the back of the head are russet or orange-brown. The sides of the head are reddish brown, blending into the black underparts. Juveniles are uniform grey-brown in colour. The wings in both adults and juveniles are dark brown.

DISTRIBUTION Distribution: Brunei, southern Cambodia, Indonesia (Bali, Java, Kalimantan, Sumatra), Malaysia (Peninsular Malaysia, Sabah, Sarawak), southern Myanmar, Philippines, Singapore, Thailand and southern Vietnam. Also found in Timor-Leste.

HABITS AND HABITAT Found in primary and secondary forest, often in mangroves and nipah palm. While sometimes found in disturbed forests, they prefer undisturbed and riparian forest. Found up to at least 1,250m. These giant bats roost high up in large trees that they often strip of foliage, in colonies from a few dozen up to 100,000 individuals. Sometimes roosts with other species. In many parts of its range populations have been greatly reduced, or completely eliminated, largely due to hunting.

NOTES The Large Flying-fox feeds on a wide range of wild and cultivated fruits (especially figs), flowers and leaves, and it is an extremely important pollinator for many trees that are valuable to local communities and for commerce, including durian.

Spotted-winged Fruit Bat ■ *Balionycteris maculata*

HB 5.3–6.2cm, T absent, FA 4–4.5cm

DESCRIPTION One of the smallest fruit bats in Asia. Dark blackish brown, with an even darker head. The underparts are grey, and it lacks an external tail. Its wing membrane is dark brown, flecked with small whitish spots, especially on the joints, and it has pale spots on the muzzle of its dog-like face, just in front of each eye. The nostrils are elongated, almost tube-like.

DISTRIBUTION Brunei, Indonesia (Kalimantan, Sumatra), Malaysia (Peninsular Malaysia, Sabah, Sarawak) and southern Thailand.

HABITS AND HABITAT Found in primary lowland forests, and occasionally montane forests, from sea level up to 1,500m. In some parts of its range it has been recorded from secondary forests. It roosts in small groups in the crowns of palms, cavities in epiphytic plants, tree-hollows, and cavities in arboreal insect nests. Gives birth to a single young up to twice a year.

NOTES The Spotted-winged Fruit Bat is threatened throughout its range by habitat loss.

ABOVE: *Four Spotted-winged Fruit Bats roosting together*

Lesser Short-nosed Fruit Bat ■ *Cynopterus brachyotis*
HB 7–8cm, T 0.8–1cm, FA 6–7cm

DESCRIPTION A moderately small fruit bat. Brown to yellowish brown with an orange collar. The collar is more yellowish in colour in females. Pale edges to the ears, and whitish wing bones visible through translucent skin. Has a broad snout.

DISTRIBUTION Cambodia, Indonesia (Java, Kalimantan, Sumatra), Laos, Malaysia (Peninsular Malaysia, Sabah, Sarawak), Myanmar, Philippines, Singapore, Thailand and Vietnam. Presence in Brunei uncertain. Also found in China, India, Sri Lanka and Timor-Leste.

HABITS AND HABITAT Lowland primary and secondary forests, mangroves, orchards, parks and gardens. It roosts in palms, under shaded trees, or near cave entrances in rural and urban landscapes and in forested areas, either solitary or in small groups. It feeds on small fruits, figs and nectar.

NOTES The taxonomy of this species is yet to be clarified, and it may in fact represent a number of species.

Cave Nectar Bat ▪ *Eonycteris spelaea* HB 8.5–11cm, T 1.5–1.8cm, FA 6–7cm

DESCRIPTION Upperparts grey-brown to dark brown. Underparts paler. Neck sometimes yellowish brown. The muzzle is elongated, adapted for drinking nectar. Short external tail.

DISTRIBUTION Brunei, Cambodia, Indonesia (Java, Kalimantan, Sumatra), Laos, Malaysia (Peninsular Malaysia, Sabah, Sarawak), Myanmar, Philippines, Singapore, Thailand and Vietnam. Also found in China, India and Timor-Leste.

HABITS AND HABITAT Found in primary forests and in disturbed and agricultural areas. Roosts in caves, in large groups, with some roosts exceeding 50,000 individuals. Sometimes roosts with other bat species. In some places, this species seems to have adapted well to leafy, semi-urban habitats. Travels many kilometres each night in search of the nectar of flowering trees and shrubs.

NOTES This species is an important pollinator of fruit trees, such as durian.

Leschenault's Rousette ▪ *Rousettus leschenaultii*
HB 9.5–12cm, T 1–1.8cm, FA 7.5–8.5cm

DESCRIPTION Brown to grey-brown in colour with lighter underparts. Long pale hairs under the chin. Elongated muzzle and large dark eyes.

DISTRIBUTION Cambodia, Indonesia (Bali, Java, Sumatra), Laos, Malaysia (Peninsular Malaysia), Myanmar, Thailand and Vietnam. Also found in Bangladesh, Bhutan, China, India, Nepal, Pakistan and Sri Lanka.

HABITS AND HABITAT Found in a variety of habitats ranging from tropical forests to urban environments, roosting in caves, old abandoned buildings and tunnels, and other such structures. Roosts in colonies of up to several thousand individuals. Feeds on fruits, nectar and flowers.

NOTES As with other rousettes, it clicks its tongue audibly for echolocation, which is a more primitive form of echolocation, compared to the more sophisticated form where ultrasonic pulses come from vocalisations produced in the larynx.

Greater False-vampire ■ *Megaderma lyra*

HB 6.5–9.5cm, T absent, FA 6.5–7.2cm

DESCRIPTION Upperparts greyish brown with long fur. Underparts paler. No visible tail. Very large ears, joined at the base. Posterior lobe of noseleaf elongate with stiffened central ridge, approximately parallel-sided flaps on the sides and squared off at the top. Intermediate noseleaf is narrower than the anterior noseleaf. Anterior noseleaf does not cover the protruding muzzle.

DISTRIBUTION Cambodia, Laos, Malaysia (Peninsular Malaysia), Myanmar, Thailand and Vietnam. Also found in Afghanistan, Bangladesh, China, India, Nepal, Pakistan and Sri Lanka.

HABITS AND HABITAT Found in a variety of habitats, including arid lands, humid forests and coastal areas. Gleans prey from branches or the ground, including large insects, and small vertebrates, such as lizards, small mammals and birds. Roosts in caves as well as man-made structures.

NOTES This species does not drink blood, unlike true vampire bats from the Americas.

Great Roundleaf Bat ▪ *Hipposideros armiger*

HB 8.5–10cm, T 5.4–6.9cm, FA 8.5–10cm

DESCRIPTION Roundleaf bats are insectivorous bats, known for having an elaborate noseleaf. The Great Roundleaf Bat is dark brown, sometimes with a paler underside. Ears, wings and noseleaf are dark brown. Similar in appearance to the closely related, but smaller, Intermediate Roundleaf Bat (p. 26), this species possesses four, not three, lateral accessory leaflets on each side of the main noseleaf. Males have a fleshy, swollen area above and behind the noseleaf. Males are larger than females. The tip of the tail is free.

DISTRIBUTION Cambodia, Laos, Malaysia (Peninsular Malaysia), Myanmar, Thailand and Vietnam. Also found in China, India, Hong Kong, Nepal and Taiwan.

HABITS AND HABITAT Usually found at higher altitudes. Found in primary and secondary forests. Roosts in caves, cracks in rocks and old buildings, alone or in colonies numbering in the hundreds, sometimes with other species.

NOTES Sometimes found high in open skies, possibly moving between roosting and foraging locations.

Intermediate Roundleaf Bat ■ *Hipposideros larvatus*

HB 6–8cm, T 3–4.5cm, FA 5–6.5cm

DESCRIPTION Dark grey-brown or reddish brown, underparts slightly paler. Ears and noseleaf dark grey or brown. Three lateral leaflets on each side of the noseleaf. The ears are broad and triangular.

DISTRIBUTION Cambodia, Indonesia (Bali, Java, Kalimantan, Sumatra), Laos, Malaysia (Peninsular Malaysia, Sabah, Sarawak), Myanmar, Thailand and Vietnam. Also found in Bangladesh, China and India.

HABITS AND HABITAT Found in a variety of habitats from primary and secondary forests to highly disturbed agricultural land, often associated with limestone caves. Roosts in caves, abandoned mines and rock crevices, sometimes in large numbers.

NOTES The taxonomy of this species remains to be clarified, and it may represent a number of species.

Rickett's Myotis ■ *Myotis pilosus* HB 6.5cm, T 5–5.5cm, FA 5.3–5.6cm

DESCRIPTION Vesper bats, also known as evening or common bats, are the most diverse and widespread bat family. In South-East Asia, vesper bats have simple noses. The upperparts of this species are buffy grey-brown, with darker bases to the hairs. Underparts greyish white. Enormous feet with long curved claws. The wing membrane is attached at the ankles.

DISTRIBUTION Laos and Vietnam. Also found in China.

HABITS AND HABITAT Found along rocky streams near limestone. Very little is known of the roosting sites of this species, but it likely uses caves.

NOTES This bat uses its extremely large feet to catch prey from the water, including small fish.

Great Evening Bat ■ *Ia io* HB 8.9–10.4cm, T 6–8.3cm, FA 7–8cm

DESCRIPTION Upperparts are sooty brown in colour, and the underparts are greyish brown. The face is mostly hairless. It has short ears with dense fur inside close to the tips. The tail extends only slightly beyond the interfemoral membrane.

DISTRIBUTION Cambodia, Laos, Myanmar, Thailand and Vietnam. Also found in China, India and Nepal.

HABITS AND HABITAT Found in primary tropical forests, typically in limestone karst areas, although in Vietnam it is found in non-limestone areas. It is a cave-roosting species and has been recorded at elevations of 200–1,700m.

NOTES The largest known population in South-East Asia is in Thailand, where roosts of up to about 20 individuals have been recorded.

Lesser Asian House Bat ▪ *Scotophilus kuhlii*

HB 6.7–7.2cm, T 3.9–5.3cm, FA 4.5–5.2cm

DESCRIPTION Upperparts brown and underparts paler yellowish brown, sometime with an orange tinge. A dog-like face with a blunt muzzle. Large pointed ears. The tail is long and enclosed in the membrane between the hind legs.

DISTRIBUTION Cambodia, Indonesia (Bali, Java, Sumatra), Laos, Malaysia (Peninsular Malaysia, Sabah), Myanmar, Philippines, Thailand and Vietnam. Also found in Bangladesh, China, Hong Kong, India, Pakistan, Sri Lanka, Taiwan and Timor-Leste.

HABITS AND HABITAT Found in primary and secondary habitats, and in both rural and urban areas. It roosts in caves, hollow trees, palm fronds and in old buildings, often in colonies of several hundred. Feeds on aerial insects in open areas.

NOTES Can be observed at night, hunting insects in flight in wooded areas as well as in towns and cities.

> **LORISES**
> Lorises are small, stocky nocturnal primates with forward-facing eyes and a vestigial tail. Their hands appear human-like with opposable thumbs. They are related to lemurs, pottos and bushbabies and are considered amongst the more primitive primates.

Bornean Slow Loris ▪ *Nycticebus menagensis* HB 26–38cm, T 1–2cm

DESCRIPTION The Bornean Slow Loris has pale golden to red fur, with almost no markings on the head. A round head, very short ears. Like other lorises, it has large round eyes. This is the smallest of the Indonesian slow lorises, and until recently was considered a subspecies of the Sunda Slow Loris (p. 33).

DISTRIBUTION Endemic to Borneo: Brunei, Indonesia (Kalimantan), Malaysia (Sabah, Sarawak) and Philippines.

HABITS AND HABITAT Found in both primary and secondary lowland forest as well as gardens and plantations. Like all lorises, it is nocturnal and almost completely arboreal. It is omnivorous, eating the gum from woody vegetation as well insects and animal matter. Detailed information on its diet is lacking, but research is ongoing.

NOTES Lorises are the only venomous primates. The venom is secreted by glands on the insides of their elbows. The animal licks the gland, and once the secretion is mixed with saliva its bite becomes lethal to its prey.

Javan Slow Loris ■ *Nycticebus javanicus* HB 30–39cm, T 1–2cm

DESCRIPTION Once considered a subspecies of the Sunda Slow Loris (p. 33), the Javan Slow Loris is now recognised as its own species, making it endemic for the Indonesian island of Java. Its fur is yellowish brown, with a dark dorsal stripe. The head, shoulders and neck are paler. It has a prominent creamy-white diamond shape between its eyes, formed by a distinct stripe that starts at the top of its head and forks towards its eyes and ears, extending down to its cheeks. It has dark fur on its ears.

DISTRIBUTION Indonesia (Java).

HABITS AND HABITAT Nocturnal and arboreal, moving slowly between hanging vines and branches like other lorises. It is found in both primary and secondary disturbed forest. Its main diet is the gum of trees, as well as insects. It sleeps curled up in branches.

NOTES This species is frequently a victim of the illegal pet trade in Indonesia.

Pygmy Loris ■ *Nycticebus pygmaeus* HB 21–29cm, T 1–2cm

DESCRIPTION Thick and short woolly fur that is light brownish grey to orange and reddish brown, with silver frosting. Underparts are light grey and the ears are relatively conspicuous. The dorsal stripe is often faint or absent but it can be bold on some individuals at some times of year. The large eyes, a defining characteristic of all lorises, are encircled with dark rings.

DISTRIBUTION Cambodia, Laos and Vietnam, only east of the Mekong. Presence in China uncertain.

HABITS AND HABITAT Primary evergreen and semi-evergreen forest, limestone forest, bamboo, secondary and even highly degraded habitats. Nocturnal and arboreal. Forages alone, eating mainly insects and gum as well as other plant matter and small animal prey such as geckos and birds.

NOTES Like other lorises, it has a nail on each digit of its hands and feet, but the nail on the second digit on each foot is shaped more like a claw and is used in grooming.

Sunda Slow Loris ■ *Nycticebus coucang* HB 26–30cm, T 1.5–2.5cm

DESCRIPTION The fur colour varies from light grey-brown to reddish brown, with a dark dorsal stripe that extends from the top of the head to the lower back. On the back of the neck this stripe branches into four lines connecting to the ears and eyes. The large eyes are encircled by dark rings.

DISTRIBUTION Indonesia (Sumatra), Malaysia (Peninsular Malaysia), Singapore and Thailand.

HABITS AND HABITAT It is found in primary and secondary lowland forest, as well as gardens and plantations. Like other lorises, it is nocturnal and almost exclusively arboreal. It is mainly frugivorous, but also consumes nectar gum and sap as well as insects, birds' eggs and leaves.

> **TARSIERS**
> At a glance, tarsiers look similar to lorises and even lemurs, but they are not closely related. Very small size and large round eyes are its most notable features. It has long bony fingers and toes, with pads on the tips. Its relatively large ears are almost furless.

Western Tarsier ▪ *Tarsius bancanus* HB 12–15cm, T 18–22cm

DESCRIPTION Colour varies with subspecies, the one on Borneo (*T. b. bancanus*) being more golden orange and rusty brown than the others, which are more ivory-yellow.

It has a tuft of long hair at the end of its very long and otherwise hairless tail.

DISTRIBUTION Brunei, Indonesia (Kalimantan, Sumatra) and Malaysia (Sabah, Sarawak).

HABITS AND HABITAT Nocturnal and arboreal. Primary and secondary forest, and also forest edge and along coasts. Exclusive diet of animal prey, consuming mainly insects such as beetles, grasshoppers, butterflies, moths and ants. Also takes small vertebrates such as birds, bats and snakes. Infants weigh a mere 25g at birth, but grow rapidly, catching their own insect prey at 4 weeks of age. Clings vertically, leaping between trees to capture prey and move about. Forages low in trees, around 2m off the ground, but if frightened it will retreat to greater heights.

NOTES It can jump up to 5m or more from tree to tree, which is about 40 times its head and body length. Like all tarsiers, it can also rotate its head nearly 180°, giving it an extremely wide field of vision.

> **MONKEYS**
> Old World monkeys do not have the prehensile tail found in New World species.
> Monkeys in South-East Asia are broadly split into colobines (langurs and relatives)
> and macaques.

Thomas's Langur ■ *Presbytis thomasi* HB 42–61cm, T 50–85cm

DESCRIPTION Thomas's Langur has strikingly beautiful facial markings. The eyes are
surrounded by white and grey-blue, and it has a grey crest flanked by two white stripes,
with a black moustache and a flesh-coloured muzzle. The upperparts (back and upper sides
of limbs) are grey, the underparts are white, and it has a very long pale tail. The hands and
feet are black.

DISTRIBUTION Indonesia (Sumatra). Endemic only to the two provinces of Aceh and
North Sumatra.

HABITS AND HABITAT Primary and secondary rainforest and neighbouring rubber tree
plantations. Feeds mainly on young leaves, fruit and flowers but will also take small animal
matter. Lives in family groups, usually of several females and one male, but small groups of
males, or even solitary males, have been observed. Mainly arboreal but occasionally comes
down to the ground to feed.

NOTES There are good places to spot this species near the Bohorok Orangutan Centre in
Bukit Lawang and in the Gunung Leuser National Park.

White-thighed Langur ■ *Presbytis siamensis* HB 43–69cm, T 68–84cm

DESCRIPTION Langurs have large, sacculated stomachs with many chambers. This is an important adaptation that allows for the breaking down of leafy material, which is the main diet, into digestible matter. Langurs are also referred to as leaf monkeys because of this dietary preference. The White-thighed Langur has brown to greyish-brown upperparts and top of head and arms, black hands, feet and distal half of tail, and pale grey underside of body, arms and legs including large patch on outer thighs. Facial skin is dark grey to almost black, and occasionally the skin around the eyes is paler. Looks very similar to the Common Banded Langur (p. 37), but that species lacks the pale outer thighs.

DISTRIBUTION Indonesia (Sumatra), Malaysia (Peninsular Malaysia) and southernmost Thailand.

HABITS AND HABITAT Lowland to hill forests, including disturbed forests and plantations. Diurnal and arboreal.

NOTES Not much is known about this species, as until recently it was considered a subspecies of the Common Banded Langur. There is still some uncertainty regarding these two species, which only further research will clarify.

Common Banded Langur ▪ *Presbytis femoralis* HB 46–59cm, T 69–77cm

DESCRIPTION Dark brown to blackish upperparts, grey underparts with pale patches on inner thighs. Grey crest, pale grey skin around eyes but not light enough to give the appearance of 'spectacles', in contrast to the Dusky Langur (p. 41).

DISTRIBUTION Indonesia (Sumatra), Malaysia (Peninsular Malaysia), Myanmar, Singapore and Thailand.

HABITS AND HABITAT Diurnal and arboreal. Diet of young leaves and fruit. Wide variety of habitats, from mixed mangrove to primary and secondary forest.

NOTES The animals that are found in Singapore are thought to belong to a distinct subspecies, but this is as yet unconfirmed. There is a small population of approximately 40 individuals in one site, at the Central Catchment Nature Reserve.

Maroon Langur ■ *Presbytis rubicunda* HB 44–58cm, T 67–80cm

DESCRIPTION The fur of this leaf monkey is reddish brown (similar in colour to an orangutan, p. 54) to golden-brown, and its face has a bluish tinge. Five subspecies exist, with slightly varying fur colouration. *P. r. chrysea*, which occurs in a small area near the Kinabatangan River in Sabah, is paler golden-brown, whereas the others are generally more reddish brown. One of the subspecies occurring in Kalimantan, *P. r. rubicunda*, has blackish extremities to its limbs.

DISTRIBUTION Endemic to Borneo: Indonesia (Kalimantan) and Malaysia (Sabah, Sarawak). Presence in Brunei uncertain.

HABITS AND HABITAT Prefers primary and secondary lowland to swamp forests, and also visits gardens to feed. Mainly arboreal. Mainly young leaves, seeds, fruits and flowers, but its diet does vary according to the availability of food sources. It lives in groups of up to 13, and males use loud calls to mark their territories.

NOTES This species is fairly common and widely distributed, and is the least threatened Bornean colobine, though numbers are probably decreasing – mainly from habitat loss.

Hose's Langur ■ *Presbytis hosei* HB 48–56cm, T 65–84cm

DESCRIPTION Relatively small with a slim build, a high forehead and a prominent crest. The different subspecies have different fur colours, but predominantly they have grey fur on their backs with white underparts and blackish hands and feet. The facial skin is pink, with bold black markings in some subspecies.

DISTRIBUTION Endemic to Borneo: Brunei, Indonesia (Kalimantan) and Malaysia (Sabah, Sarawak).

HABITS AND HABITAT Lowland to hill dipterocarp rainforest. Its main diet is leaves, and also flowers, fruits, seeds, birds' eggs and nestlings. Sympatric with Maroon Langur (p. 38), sometimes associating closely with this species, which is unusual for Asian colobines. It is diurnal and arboreal, mainly occupying the mid-level of the forest canopy and coming down to the ground to visit salt licks.

Sundaic Silvered Langur ■ *Trachypithecus cristatus*

HB 41–54cm, T 60–76cm

DESCRIPTION Overall dark grey with pale grey frosting, dark grey face and pointed crest. Infants are bright orange, but patches of grey appear as they grow, until they adopt the full adult colouration. Long limbs and very long tail, which aids in balance as the animal moves through the trees. Males and females look similar, but males are larger.

DISTRIBUTION Brunei, Indonesia (Kalimantan, Sumatra) and Malaysia (Peninsular Malaysia, Sabah, Sarawak).

HABITS AND HABITAT Diurnal and arboreal. Coastal, riverine and mangrove swamp forests. Diet of mainly young leaves, shoots, flowers, seeds and fruit, especially mangrove species. As in other leaf monkeys, its large sacculated stomach allows it to process its leafy diet, which it consumes in large volumes. Lives in groups of between 10 and 50 individuals.

NOTES In Malaysia, fantastic viewing opportunities are available at the Kuala Selangor Nature Park, where there are several large family groups.

Dusky Langur ■ *Trachypithecus obscurus* HB 50–70cm, T 70–80cm

DESCRIPTION Distinct face, with incomplete white rings around the eyes against dark grey facial skin, giving it the appearance of spectacles – hence its other common name, the Spectacled Langur. Greyish-brown to dark grey upperparts with paler grey outer hind legs, tail and crest. Bare pink patches on the lips. Infants are light orange.

DISTRIBUTION Malaysia (Peninsular Malaysia, Sabah, Sarawak), Myanmar and Thailand.

HABITS AND HABITAT Mainly arboreal. Lives in a variety of habitat, from lowland to hills. Main diet of leaves, shoots and some unripe fruit. It is usually found in groups of between five and twenty.

Javan Langur ■ *Trachypithecus auratus* HB 50–70cm, T 70–80cm

DESCRIPTION This species has a small crest, and the fur encircling its face points forward. Facial skin has a bluish tinge and it has prominent cheek tufts. The most common form is the black morph. One population, with a very restricted distribution between Blitar, Ijen and Pugeran in Java, is reddish brown.

DISTRIBUTION Indonesia (Bali, Java).

HABITS AND HABITAT Diurnal and arboreal. Mangrove and freshwater swamp forests, lowland and montane forests up to 3,000–3,500m. Diet of mainly leaves, flowers, fruit seeds and unripe fruit.

NOTES This Indonesian endemic is threatened by a host of factors, especially habitat loss and degradation as a result of agricultural and residential expansion, as well as poaching for its meat and to supply the pet trade.

Hatinh Langur ■ *Trachypithecus hatinhensis* HB 50–66cm, T 81–87cm

DESCRIPTION Glossy black fur covers the whole body, except for a white moustache extending from the sides of its mouth over its ears to the nape of its neck. It has a distinct black crest. Juveniles have a white band on their foreheads, which disappears when they reach adulthood. It is fairly similar to the François' Langur (*Trachypithecus francoisi*) and the Lao Langur (*Trachypithecus laotum*), but the distinguishing characteristics are that the former's moustache does not continue behind its ears and the latter has a white forehead even in adulthood.

DISTRIBUTION Vietnam (central). Possibly in adjacent Laos.

HABITS AND HABITAT Spends considerable time in trees and on the ground. Its main diet is leaves. Found in forests near limestone karsts and outcrops in rocky mountainous areas, though its previous range may have included a wider habitat variety.

Capped Langur ■ *Trachypithecus pileatus* HB 50–70cm, T 80–100cm

DESCRIPTION Distinct black cap and dark face, with facial hair and underparts pale yellow to orange. Hairs on crown are short, sticking straight up. Grey to pale brown body and tail, with black tip to tail. Easy to distinguish from other langurs, as none of the others has such a dark cap contrasting with yellow-orange cheeks. Juveniles up to the age of 5 months are creamy-white with a pink face.

DISTRIBUTION Myanmar (north-west). Also found in Bangladesh, Bhutan and India.

HABITS AND HABITAT Evergreen, semi-evergreen, moist deciduous forest, bamboo and open woodlands. Diurnal and largely arboreal, eats mainly leaves and also fruit, seeds and flowers. Lives in groups of multiple females with one male.

Red-shanked Douc ■ *Pygathrix nemaeus* HB 61–76cm, T 56–76cm

DESCRIPTION A strikingly colourful large primate. Dark reddish-chestnut lower legs, black hands, feet, shoulders, insides of upper arms, upper legs and rump, with white lower arms and speckled grey back, belly and tops of upper arms. It has a yellow-brown face and a long white tail.

DISTRIBUTION Laos and Vietnam. Possibly in small part of adjacent Cambodia.

HABITS AND HABITAT Tall evergreen and semi-evergreen primary forest, lowlands up to 2,000m, including limestone outcrops. Mainly arboreal, feeds on leaves and buds, and some fruit, flowers and seeds.

NOTES When relaxed, these monkeys move noisily in the trees, disappearing quietly only when disturbed.

Black-shanked Douc ■ *Pygathrix nigripes* HB 61–76cm, T 56–76cm

DESCRIPTION Dark speckled grey crown and upperparts, paler grey underparts, white chin and throat, black limbs with paler frosting on arms. Blue-grey skin on face, yellow-orange eye-rings, and a long white tail.

DISTRIBUTION Cambodia and Vietnam.

HABITS AND HABITAT Evergreen, semi-evergreen and mixed deciduous forest. Mainly arboreal. Feeds on leaves and seeds, and some fruit, flowers and buds.

Proboscis Monkey ■ *Nasalis larvatus* HB 55–65cm, T 62–75cm

DESCRIPTION A very large primate, with its most distinctive characteristics being the oversized nose and stomach of the adult male. Males are larger than females. It has reddish-brown fur with greyish limbs. Females and young have small, upturned noses.

DISTRIBUTION Brunei, Indonesia (Kalimantan) and Malaysia (Sabah, Sarawak).

HABITS AND HABITAT Riparian-riverine forests, coastal lowland forest, including mangroves, peat-swamp, and freshwater swamp forest. Main diet of young leaves and unripe fruit.

NOTES Good viewing opportunities along the Kinabatangan River in Sabah. They have partly webbed hind feet, which aid in balancing on mangrove mud and swimming – they swim with dog-paddle-like movements.

Southern Pig-tailed Macaque ■ *Macaca nemestrina*

HB 47–59cm, T 14–23cm

DESCRIPTION Macaques are geographically more widespread than any other group of primates, except humans, with 21 species currently recognised. Macaques generally have bare skin on their faces and bottoms. The Southern Pig-tailed Macaque is a stocky, heavy-set macaque with a short curly tail. It has an olive-brown coat, with a dark brown crown and whitish underparts.

DISTRIBUTION Brunei, Indonesia (Kalimantan, Sumatra), Malaysia (Peninsular Malaysia, Sabah, Sarawak) and peninsular Thailand.

HABITS AND HABITAT Diurnal. Eats fruit and small animals. Usually lives in large groups of between 15 and 40 individuals, but males are sometimes solitary. It often descends to the ground to flee from danger.

NOTES A closely related species is the Northern Pig-tailed Macaque (*Macaca leonina*), which is very similar, but of lighter build. It occurs in Bangladesh, Cambodia, China, India, Laos, Myanmar, Thailand (mainland) and Vietnam – and with the slight overlap in range there is some hybridisation.

Long-tailed Macaque ■ *Macaca fascicularis* HB 45–55cm, T 44–55cm

DESCRIPTION This species has grey-brown to reddish-brown fur, with slightly paler undersides. Its face is brownish grey with cheek whiskers. It has a lean build, with males being significantly larger than females. It has a long tail.

DISTRIBUTION Brunei, Cambodia, Indonesia, Laos, Malaysia, Myanmar, Philippines, Singapore, Thailand and Vietnam. Also in Bangladesh, India (Andaman and Nicobar Islands) and Timor-Leste.

HABITS AND HABITAT It is a gregarious primate, often congregating in groups of 20–30. It is especially common near coastal areas and forest edges, often near people. It is an omnivore, eating a wide range of animal matter and vegetation and is diurnal, sleeping in the branches of trees during the night.

NOTES People often feed them, especially in tourist spots, and this is heavily discouraged as it alters their behaviour, and can make them aggressive and overly dependent on people. As a result, aggressive macaques are frequently killed.

Siamang ▪ *Symphalangus syndactylus* HB 75–90cm, T absent

DESCRIPTION Gibbons have a distinct slender form, with long forelimbs, short hind limbs. This body shape is a special adaptation for moving (brachiating) through the forest. The Siamang is the largest of the gibbons. It has shaggy black hair, with a greyish lower face, no tail, and a throat pouch that is visibly inflated when calling.

DISTRIBUTION Indonesia (Sumatra), Malaysia (Peninsular Malaysia) and southernmost Thailand.

HABITS AND HABITAT It is arboreal but less gregarious than other gibbons, brachiating gracefully through the trees. Found in primary and secondary forest, from lowlands up to 1,500m. Found in small family groups, typically of a pair with their offspring.

NOTES Loud booming call, followed by a whooping 'hoo' call. Male calls end with a very loud yell. Fraser's Hill in Malaysia offers good chances of seeing these animals.

White-handed Gibbon ▪ *Hylobates lar* HB 45–60cm, T absent

DESCRIPTION Two colour forms, blonde and dark brown, can occur in the same family, unrelated to sex. It has long limbs, with white feet and hands. It has a pale ring around its face and has no tail.

DISTRIBUTION Indonesia (Sumatra), northern Laos (west of Mekong), Malaysia (Peninsular Malaysia), Myanmar, Thailand. Possibly extinct in China (Yunnan).

HABITS AND HABITAT Arboreal, travelling rapidly through the trees by swinging from its arms. Loud and distinct high-pitched whooping call. Often seen dangling from branches or huddled in forks of trees. Largely frugivorous, but also eats young shoots and leaves, and insects.

NOTES In Thailand, the largest population is in Kaeng Krachan National Park, which offers good viewing (and definitely hearing) opportunities. These gibbons are important seed dispersers, as they swallow nearly all the seeds in their food.

Agile Gibbon ▪

Hylobates agilis
HB 45–65cm, T absent

DESCRIPTION There are two colour forms, buff-blonde and very dark-brown, unrelated to sex. The dark phase is generally more common in mainland South-East Asia. Similar to White-handed Gibbon (p. 51) but with pale brow and cheeks and an incomplete ring, and it also lacks the pale hands and feet.

DISTRIBUTION Indonesia (Sumatra), Malaysia (Peninsular Malaysia) and southernmost Thailand.

HABITS AND HABITAT Arboreal. Found in small family groups. Tall dipterocarp forests. Peak calling time after dawn.

NOTES Call similar to White-handed Gibbon, but shorter duration and more of a 'whoo-aa' call.

Müller's Bornean Gibbon ▪ *Hylobates muelleri*

HB 42–47cm, T absent

DESCRIPTION Fur colour varies from grey to brown, with the top of the head and the chest being darker.

DISTRIBUTION Brunei, Indonesia (Kalimantan) and Malaysia (Sabah, Sarawak).

HABITS AND HABITAT Found in primary and secondary forest, also in selectively logged forest. It is arboreal, moving rapidly in the trees, and diurnal. It favours high-sugar fleshy fruit, but also eats young leaves and small insects.

Hoolock ▪ *Hoolock hoolock* HB 45–65cm, T absent

DESCRIPTION Males are largely black, with thick white eyebrows, occasionally with a white tuft on the chin. Females have a buff-brown colouring.

DISTRIBUTION Myanmar. Also found in Bangladesh and India. Presence in China uncertain.

HABITS AND HABITAT Primary and semi-evergreen forest. Arboreal, diurnal. Fruits, leaves and shoots are the main diet.

NOTES Sometimes considered two separate species; the Eastern Hoolock (*H. leuconedys*) occurs on the east of Chindwin River in Myanmar, and in southern China while the Western Hoolock (*H. hoolock*) is found west of the Chindwin River in Myanmar, Bangladesh and India.

ORANGUTANS
Orangutans are Asia's only great apes. The Sumatran Orangutan was formerly considered a subspecies of the Bornean Orangutan, but recent research has confirmed that Borneo holds one species and Sumatra another.

Sumatran Orangutan ▪ *Pongo abelii*
Bornean Orangutan ▪ *Pongo pygmaeus* HB 78–97cm, T absent

DESCRIPTION The two species are very similar in appearance. Large, with a reddish-brown shaggy coat, long limbs and no tail. They have bare, dark facial skin, though juveniles have pinkish faces. Males are much larger than females. The Bornean Orangutan has a broader face with less facial hair, and appears darker overall than the Sumatran Orangutan.

ABOVE AND OPPOSITE PAGE, TOP: *Sumatran Orangutan*

DISTRIBUTION Sumatran Orangutan in Indonesia (Sumatra); Bornean Orangutan in Indonesia (Kalimantan) and Malaysia (Sabah, Sarawak).

HABITS AND HABITAT Diet of fruit, leaves, animal prey. Consumes over 200 plant species. Primary and tall secondary forests, lowland swamp to montane forest, preferring altitudes below 500m. Males are solitary, females with offspring. Diurnal, usually arboreal.

NOTES Orangutans sleep in nests fashioned out of broken branches woven together high in the trees. They also use tools to a certain extent, such as shielding themselves from rain with leaves. One population of Sumatran Orangutans has been observed to strip branches and use them to extract honey or insects from inside trees.

BOTTOM, LEFT AND RIGHT: *Bornean Orangutan*

Golden Jackal ■ *Canis aureus* HB 60–80cm, T 20–25cm

DESCRIPTION Usually golden brown to tan with black-tipped hairs on the shoulders and back. The tail is bushy with a dark tip and hangs straight down, lacking the tip-curl usually seen on even the most jackal-like domestic dog. Golden Jackals have pointed ears, and blunt nails, having feet much like a domestic dog.

DISTRIBUTION Myanmar, Thailand, Cambodia, Laos and Vietnam. Also widespread through north and northeast Africa, down the Arabian Peninsula, in parts of Europe, through Central Asia and the entire Indian sub-continent, including Sri Lanka.

HABITS AND HABITAT Found in a wide variety of habitats throughout its range. In South-East Asia, it occupies lowland, open, decidous forest and grasslands. It can cope with some human disturbance, although in many parts of its range it is hunted as a pest or caught in indiscriminate snares and traps.

NOTES Most often seen along forest edges, in clearings or along trails. In areas where prey is abundant and threats are minimal, it occurs at higher densities and may be easier to see.

Dhole ■ *Cuon alpinus* HB 80–105cm, T 30–45cm

DESCRIPTION Reddish brown with a paler underside and a bushy tail that becomes increasingly dark to black towards the tip. The ears are rounded with white hairs inside. This is the largest of South-East Asia's wild dog species.

DISTRIBUTION Cambodia, Indonesia (Java, Sumatra), Laos, Malaysia (Peninsular Malaysia), Myanmar, Thailand and Vietnam. Also found in India, north to Russia (southern Siberia). Current distribution is highly fragmented, and this species is now absent from many parts of historical range.

HABITS AND HABITAT Found living and hunting in packs, it uses a variety of habitats, including primary and secondary forests, grassland–scrub–forest mosaics and montane forests. It hunts a wide variety of prey, including large mammals such as deer.

NOTES Very little is known about its status, distribution and ecological needs in South-East Asia, and more research is needed. Habitat loss, loss of prey, persecution and accidental snaring/trapping are some of the main threats to the continued survival of this beautiful dog.

Sun Bear ▪ *Helarctos malayanus* HB 110–140cm, T 3–7cm

DESCRIPTION The Sun Bear is the smallest of the world's bears. It has dark brown to black short fur, with a lighter brown muzzle and a large white to yellowish marking, often V-shaped, on the chest. This marking varies from one individual to the next. Ears are small and rounded. The claws are very long, powerful and non-retractable. Females are generally 10–20% smaller than males.

DISTRIBUTION Brunei, Cambodia, Indonesia (Kalimantan, Sumatra), Laos, Malaysia (Peninsular Malaysia, Sabah, Sarawak), Myanmar, Thailand and Vietnam. Also found in Bangladesh, China and India. Extinct in Singapore.

HABITS AND HABITAT In Indonesia (Sumatra) and Malaysia, it is found in dense tropical rainforest, including lowland forests, swampy areas, hills, limestone karst hills, and lower montane forest. While it can use selectively logged forests and other disturbed areas, there is no evidence that it can survive in deforested or agricultural land. It climbs extremely well and frequently builds nests in trees to sleep in. It does not hibernate.

NOTES The Sun Bear has been extirpated from many parts of its range, largely due to hunting and habitat loss, and its distribution has become increasingly patchy. The two greatest threats are habitat loss and hunting for commercial trade in its body parts, which are used in traditional Asian medicines. Further research is needed to assess the current status and conservation needs of this species. Reducing the trade in bear parts is of paramount importance.

Asian Black Bear ■ *Ursus thibetanus* HB 120–150cm, T 6–10cm

DESCRIPTION Usually uniformly black, though sometimes brown (a golden-brown colour phase has been observed in Cambodia), with a lighter brown muzzle and a distinctive creamy-white to yellowish marking across its chest, extending from shoulder to shoulder. Its coat is somewhat shaggy in appearance, compared to the shorter fur of the Sun Bear, especially on its neck. It has relatively large rounded ears, which are much larger than the Sun Bear's. Males are considerably larger than females.

DISTRIBUTION Cambodia, Laos, Myanmar, Thailand and Vietnam. Also found in Afghanistan, Bangladesh, Bhutan, China, India, Iran, Japan, North and South Korea, Nepal, Pakistan, Russia and Taiwan. It occupies all countries in mainland South-East Asia except Malaysia. There is wide overlap in South-East Asia with the Sun Bear (p. 58).

HABITS AND HABITAT Found in a variety of habitats, including both broadleaf and coniferous forests. Also uses secondary forests, taking advantage of fruit, berries or young bamboo shoots and other new growth. Occasionally visits agricultural areas and fruit orchards.

NOTES Threatened by habitat loss and hunting for their body parts, especially paws and gall bladders. Trade in live individuals for pets and for bear bile extraction is also a threat.

Red Panda ▪ *Ailurus fulgens* HB 51–63cm, T 28–48cm

DESCRIPTION The Red Panda has long soft fur. Its upperparts are reddish, darkest in the middle of the back, with paler underparts. The fur on the head is also paler, with white rims to the ears and dark marks under the eyes. The long bushy tail is banded with inconspicuous rings.

DISTRIBUTION Myanmar. Also found in Bhutan, China, India and Nepal.

HABITS AND HABITAT Found mainly in montane temperate forests at 1,800–4,000m with bamboo thicket understoreys. It is primarily nocturnal, sleeping on tree branches during the day. It is an efficient climber, feeding in the trees as well as on the ground, on a variety of vegetation including bamboo shoots, grasses, fruit, roots and acorns as well as insects, eggs and small invertebrates. Bamboo leaves are an especially important source of food during winter.

> **MARTENS**
> Martens are medium-sized carnivores that are closely related to weasels, otters, badgers, ferrets, minks and stoats.

Yellow-throated Marten ■ *Martes flavigula* HB 45–65cm, T 37–45cm

DESCRIPTION A long, slender body and a long tail. There are variations in coat pattern depending on geographic location. Its back colour varies from medium brown to pale yellowish brown, with darker brown to black lower back, hind legs, lower half of forelegs and tail. It has a black stripe on the side of its neck behind its ear, while the top of its head varies from black to dark brown, extending from the neck stripe. It has a pale yellowish chin, throat and chest with a darker lower belly.

DISTRIBUTION Brunei, Cambodia, Indonesia (Java, Kalimantan, Sumatra), Laos, Malaysia (Peninsular Malaysia, Sabah, Sarawak), Myanmar, Thailand and Vietnam. Also found in Bangladesh, Bhutan, China, India, Nepal, Pakistan, Russia, Taiwan, and North and South Korea.

HABITS AND HABITAT Mainly diurnal but also occasionally hunts at night. Found in a variety of habitats, both natural and disturbed. Its diet comprises a variety of animal matter including birds, snakes, lizards, insects, as well as fruit, nectar and honey. Often solitary or in pairs, but also seen in small family groups.

NOTES Its graceful bounding movements are distinctive; it moves with agility on the ground and in the trees.

> **Badgers**
> Badgers are generally stocky-bodied with short legs made for digging. Ferret badgers are the smallest members of the badger family.

Large-toothed Ferret Badger ▪ *Melogale personata*

HB 33–39cm, T 14–21cm

DESCRIPTION The Large-toothed Ferret Badger has brownish to greyish upperparts, paler underparts, occasionally with an orange tinge. Sides of the body frosted with white. White dorsal stripe extending from the back of the neck to the middle of the back, sometimes to the rump or tail. Tail is bushy and pale in colour, with the distal half being white. The head has a distinctive dark-brown to black and white pattern, and it has massive teeth. Very similar to other ferret-badgers, and difficult to distinguish in the field.

DISTRIBUTION Cambodia, Laos, Myanmar, Thailand and Vietnam. Also found in China and India.

HABITS AND HABITAT Nocturnal and terrestrial, although it occasionally climbs trees. Found in forests, grasslands, and sometimes cultivated areas. Omnivorous, feeding on a variety of invertebrates, frogs, and sometimes carcasses of small birds and mammals, eggs and fruit.

Sunda Stink-badger ▪ *Mydaus javanensis* HB 37–52cm, T 3–5cm

DESCRIPTION It has a black coat with a white dorsal stripe. The extent of the stripe varies, but it generally extends from the top of its head to its tail. It has a long muzzle and a very short tail.

DISTRIBUTION Indonesia (Java, Kalimantan, Sumatra) and Malaysia (Sabah, Sarawak). Presence in Brunei uncertain.

HABITS AND HABITAT Found in secondary forests and areas adjacent to forests. Its diet includes eggs, carrion, insects, earthworms, larvae as well as plants. It is terrestrial and nocturnal, and sleeps in burrows during the day. It uses its long muzzle and long claws to dig into soft soil in search of food.

NOTES The Sunda Stink-badger emits a strong odour from secretions of its anal gland, hence its name. Not a badger at all, this species and its close relative, the Palawan Stink-badger *Mydaus marchei* are the only two species of skunks (Mephitidae) in the Old World.

> **OTTERS**
> Otters are semi-aquatic carnivorous mammals.

Smooth Otter ■ *Lutrogale perspicillata* HB 65–75cm, T 40–45cm

DESCRIPTION The largest of Asia's four otter species, the Smooth Otter is long and sleek. Upperparts are brown, underparts slightly lighter. The throat and sides of the neck, extending from the chin to the chest, are creamy. The tail is flattened – much more so than in other Asian otter species. The head appears blunt compared with Asia's other larger otter species, and the nose is hairless. Large webbed feet.

DISTRIBUTION Brunei, Cambodia, Indonesia (Java, Kalimantan, Sumatra), Laos, Malaysia (Peninsular Malaysia, Sabah, Sarawak), Myanmar, Singapore, Thailand and Vietnam. Also found in Bangladesh, Bhutan, China, India, Iraq, Nepal and Pakistan.

HABITS AND HABITAT Diurnal, found in primary and disturbed habitats, in coastal areas such as estuaries and mangroves, and in lakes, reservoirs, ponds and large rivers. Sometimes solitary, although more often in groups of up to 15 or more, with 4–6 being the norm. Hunts cooperatively, taking a wide variety of prey including fish, crustaceans, shellfish, amphibians, reptiles and even some small mammals.

NOTES One of the more easily observed species in some parts of its range, such as Malaysia and Singapore. Various birds often follow groups of Smooth Otters as they hunt, taking advantage of the disturbed fish and the chance of an easy meal.

Oriental Small-clawed Otter ■ *Aonyx cinereus* HB 36–55cm, T 22–35cm

DESCRIPTION The smallest of the region's four otter species. Upperparts dark brown, underparts paler brown. The sides of neck and throat, the chin and cheeks are a buffy colour. The muzzle is blunt. As its name implies, it has short claws, not extending beyond the ends of the digits.

DISTRIBUTION Brunei, Cambodia, Indonesia (Java, Kalimantan, Sumatra), Laos, Malaysia (Peninsular Malaysia, Sabah, Sarawak), Myanmar, Philippines (Palawan), Singapore, Thailand and Vietnam. Also found in Bangladesh, Bhutan, China, India, Nepal and Taiwan.

HABITS AND HABITAT Largely diurnal. Occurs in a wide variety of habitats with permanent water and forest cover, including sea coasts, mangroves, rivers, streams, ponds and lakes, as well as in agricultural paddy areas. Mostly in groups of 4–15 animals, though there is little information on group composition or behaviour.

NOTES As with the other Asian otters, populations have declined throughout much of its range due to habitat loss and hunting for trade in fur, meat and body parts used in traditional medicines.

Hairy-nosed Otter ■ *Lutra sumatrana* HB 55–72cm, T 37–48cm

DESCRIPTION Large, brown with creamy chin, lips and upper parts of the throat. It has prominent claws and fully webbed digits. The head is flatter and less blunt than that of the Smooth Otter (p. 64). The unique hair-covered nose, which gives it its common name, is one of the most important features to distinguish this species from the very similar Eurasian Otter (p. 67).

DISTRIBUTION Brunei, Cambodia, Indonesia (Sumatra, Kalimantan), Malaysia (Peninsular Malaysia, Sabah, Sarawak), Thailand and Vietnam. Presence in Laos and Myanmar uncertain.

HABITS AND HABITAT Very little is known of this rare nocturnal species. It appears to be solitary in nature, but it may occur in groups of up to six. Found in coastal areas, swamps, large rivers and associated tributaries and lakes.

NOTES The Hairy-nosed Otter is severely threatened by hunting for skins, meat and medicine. More research is essential to better understand and protect this species.

Eurasian Otter ■ *Lutra lutra* HB 50–80cm, T 37–50cm

DESCRIPTION Brown upperparts with paler brown underparts. The chin and throat are lighter brown. Very similar in appearance to the Hairy-nosed Otter (p. 66), but the tip of the nose is hairless. The coat appears grizzled and rough. The head is flatter and less blunt than in the Smooth Otter (p. 64).

DISTRIBUTION Cambodia, Indonesia (Sumatra), Laos, Myanmar, Thailand and Vietnam. Also found from Europe, through North Africa, North Asia, South Asia and East Asia.

HABITS AND HABITAT Largely nocturnal, although sometimes active during the day, depending on the vulnerability of prey in daylight hours. Occurs in a wide variety of habitats, including highland and lowland lakes, rivers, streams, swamps and coastal areas, from sea-level to high in the mountains. Usually near banks with substantial covering vegetation.

While fish make up the bulk of the diet, it also eats crustaceans, aquatic insects, reptiles, amphibians, birds and small mammals. Largely solitary, although sometimes in small groups made up of mother and offspring.

NOTES In some parts of its range the distribution of the Eurasian Otter overlaps with that of Smooth Otters and Oriental Small-clawed Otters (p. 65).

> **CIVETS**
> Civets are often referred to as civet cats, but they are not felines.

Large Indian Civet ▪ *Viverra zibetha* HB 75–85cm, T 38–46cm

DESCRIPTION The Large Indian Civet is grey-brown with mottled dark spots that turn into wavy lines closer to the rump. Black erectile hairs run from the back of the neck down the back, ending at the base of the tail. The thick tail is ringed with five or six white bands, alternating with black bands. The neck is boldly marked with black and white. A sheath of skin covers the claw on the third and fourth toe.

DISTRIBUTION Cambodia, Laos, Malaysia (Peninsular Malaysia), Myanmar, Thailand and Vietnam. Also found in Bhutan, China, India and Nepal. Possibly extinct in Singapore.

HABITS AND HABITAT Found in primary and secondary forests, and occasionally in plantations or otherwise altered and degraded habitats. It has been recorded up to 1,600m, rarely below 400m, where a related species, Large-spotted Civet *Viverra megaspila*, tends to predominate. While largely terrestrial, it can climb. Feeds on a wide variety of prey, including fish, birds, lizards, frogs, insects, arthropods and crabs, as well as domestic poultry and even garbage.

NOTES While this species appears to be common across much of its range, hunting, trapping and snaring are apparently taking a toll, and as a result it is becoming increasingly rare, especially where the threat of trapping goes hand-in-hand with extensive habitat loss and fragmentation. In some areas, it is now completely absent.

Malay Civet ■ *Viverra tangalunga* HB 61–67cm, T 28–36cm

DESCRIPTION Upperparts are greyish with numerous black spots and a black dorsal stripe that runs to the tip of the tail. Underparts are whitish and there are bold black markings on the otherwise white throat. The legs are dark to black. There are about 15 black bands on the tail. Longish legs and a pointed muzzle.

DISTRIBUTION Indonesia (Kalimantan, Sumatra), Malaysia (Peninsular Malaysia, Sabah, Sarawak), Philippines and Singapore. Presumably in Brunei.

HABITS AND HABITAT Largely nocturnal, but may be crepuscular. Terrestrial, although they can climb. Found in a variety of habitats including primary and secondary forests, cultivated land, plantations and near human settlements in the proximity of forest, over a wide altitudinal range, from sea level to at least 1,200m. It is largely solitary and has an omnivorous diet. Rests during the day at ground level hidden in logs, dense brush piles or thick vegetation.

NOTES May be seen at forest edges, often near agricultural areas, orchards and gardens, in the late evening, as it forages on the ground.

Masked Palm Civet ▪ *Paguma larvata* HB 51–76cm, T 51–64cm

DESCRIPTION Colour is variable throughout the range of this species, ranging from dark brown to reddish to light brown. The tail is often dark with a white tip, but not always. It has a dark mask, ears, muzzle and legs and has white cheeks. In some populations, especially in the northern parts of South-East Asia, there is white on the top of the head running from the nose to the nape, although this is less conspicuous further south, and absent altogether in the extreme south of its range.

DISTRIBUTION Brunei, Cambodia, Indonesia (Kalimantan, Sumatra), Laos, Malaysia (Peninsular Malaysia, Sabah, Sarawak), Myanmar, Thailand and Vietnam. Also found in Bhutan, China, India (Andaman Islands) and Nepal.

HABITS AND HABITAT Nocturnal with occasional diurnal activity, and partially arboreal. Occurs in primary and secondary forests, including peat-swamp forests and disturbed areas, up to 2,500m. The omnivorous diet includes small mammals, insects and fruits. Females have up to four young per litter, with two breeding seasons per year.

NOTES This species can sometimes be observed foraging on the ground, often on trails near human settlements, in areas where hunting is minimal.

Common Palm Civet ■ *Paradoxurus hermaphroditus*

HB 42–50cm, T 33–42cm

DESCRIPTION It has a long body and short dark legs, with a dark long tail. The upperparts vary widely in colour and pattern, but often are greyish brown with three dark broken lines running down the back, and irregular dark spots along the sides, sometimes forming lines as well. The underparts are lighter grey. A broad mask-like band covers the face, including the base of the pointed muzzle and ears. The forehead is lighter grey to whitish, as are the cheeks and the fore-part of the muzzle.

DISTRIBUTION Brunei, Cambodia, Indonesia (Java, Kalimantan, Sumatra), Laos, Malaysia (Peninsular Malaysia, Sabah, Sarawak), Myanmar, Philippines, Singapore, Thailand and Vietnam. Also found in Bangladesh, Bhutan, China, India, Nepal and Sri Lanka. Possibly found in Afghanistan.

HABITS AND HABITAT Largely arboreal, crepuscular and nocturnal, it is found in a wide range of habitats including evergreen and deciduous forest (primary and secondary), as well as plantations, suburbs and even urban green-space, up to 2,400m. Adapted for forest living, yet often found in areas near humans; sleeping in barns, drains, or roofs during the day, and emerging at night to catch rodents or forage for mango, coffee, pineapples, melons and bananas. It also eats insects and molluscs.

NOTES Many subspecies have been described. *P. h. lignicolor*, endemic to the Mentawai islands, is sometimes considered a separate species. In some parts of its range this species is hunted for meat, captured for the 'civet coffee' trade and the pet trade and also persecuted as a pest.

Banded Civet ▪ *Hemigalus derbyanus* HB 45–56cm, T 25–36cm

DESCRIPTION This beautiful civet has a light golden-brown to pale brown body with distinct broad dark brown to black bands across its back and at the base of its tail. The tail is darker than the body, especially further from the base. Longitudinal stripes on the neck and to the face. The underside is lighter and without barring. Pointed face with long whiskers.

DISTRIBUTION Indonesia (Kalimantan, Sumatra), Malaysia (Peninsular Malaysia, Sabah, Sarawak), southern Myanmar and southern Thailand. Presumably in Brunei as well. Appears to be more common on Borneo than elsewhere in South-East Asia.

HABITS AND HABITAT This nocturnal ground-dwelling species has been recorded from primary lowland rainforest, but also in disturbed habitat, peat-swamp forest and acacia plantations. In Borneo, it was found at elevations up to 1,200m. Significantly less abundant in secondary or disturbed forests, and there is no clear evidence that the Banded Civet can survive in plantations.

NOTES Further study of the ecology of this species is required. Being mainly terrestrial, these animals are at risk from snares and other traps.

Owston's Civet ■ *Chrotogale owstoni* HB 51–63cm, T 38–48cm

DESCRIPTION Pale brown to light grey in colour with broad black bands across the body and the base of the tail. The underside is orangeish in males and paler, yellowish, in females. The tail is darker than the body, especially further from the base. Longitudinal stripes on the neck and face, and dark brown to black spots on the sides and down the legs. The underside is lighter and lacks barring. Elongated face with long whiskers and pointed ears.

DISTRIBUTION Laos and Vietnam. Presence in Cambodia uncertain. Also found in southern China.

HABITS AND HABITAT While little is known of this species' habitat use and general ecology, it has been recorded in lowland and montane evergreen forests, broadleaf forests over limestone, and bamboo forest. Often found in mountainous highlands, and has also been recorded from heavily degraded forest and at forest edges. The range restriction of this species in eastern Laos may be associated with the extent of wet evergreen forest in the eastern Annamites.

NOTES Little is known about the range and ecology of Owston's Civets, and further studies are required. The species is severely threatened by hunting, and is particularly vulnerable to ground-level snares and traps.

Otter Civet ▪ *Cynogale bennettii* HB 57–68cm, T 12–21cm

DESCRIPTION This civet has a dark brown coat, with faint grey grizzling and pale underparts. It has prominent white lips, very long whiskers, small ears and a faint pale spot above each eye. It has partially webbed feet.

DISTRIBUTION Brunei, Indonesia (Kalimantan, Sumatra), Malaysia (Peninsular Malaysia) and southern Thailand.

HABITS AND HABITAT This is a poorly known species, but it is thought to be largely confined to peat-swamp forests, though there are recent records from lowland dry forest. It seems to prefer lowland primary forest, and is also found in secondary forest, bamboo, and logged forest, but details on its long-term habitat use are lacking. It is semi-aquatic, assumed to hunt in and near water for fish, crabs, molluscs as well as birds and small mammals. Thought to be primarily nocturnal.

NOTES Very little is known about this species, from its ecology to its population trends, pointing to an urgent need for further study.

Binturong ■ *Arctictis binturong* HB 65–95cm, T 50–80cm

DESCRIPTION Shaggy black hair with white frosting covers this long and low-slung civet. The head is slightly paler and has round, tufted ears. It has an extremely large, thick, prehensile tail. Sometimes unfortunately referred to as a 'bearcat', although is not closely related to either bears or cats.

DISTRIBUTION Brunei, Cambodia, Indonesia (Java, Kalimantan, Sumatra), Laos, Malaysia (Peninsular Malaysia, Sabah, Sarawak), Myanmar, Philippines (Palawan), Thailand and Vietnam. Also found in Bangladesh, Bhutan, China, India and Nepal. Extinct in Singapore. Historically abundant but now uncommon or rare over much of the range.

HABITS AND HABITAT Primarily arboreal. Due to its heaviness and sluggish nature it cannot leap canopy gaps, so it often has to descend to the ground to move through the forest. Crepuscular and nocturnal, although sometimes active during the day. Confined to tall forest, where it feeds on fruits and small animals such as insects, birds, rodents and fish. In the Philippines, the species is found in primary and secondary lowland forest, including grassland–forest mosaic.

NOTES Nine subspecies have been described. Of those currently recognised, the Palawan Island population (*A. b. whitei*) is sometimes considered a distinct species. Threatened by habitat loss, but also hunted for pets and consumption.

Small-toothed Palm Civet ■ *Arctogalidia trivirgata*

HB 44–53cm, T 48–66cm

DESCRIPTION Long in appearance, with a tail longer than the body, and short legs. It is usually dark greyish brown, though sometimes slightly lighter, with slightly lighter and reddish underparts. Three black stripes run down the back. These stripes can be difficult to see, and care must be taken not to confuse this species with Common Palm Civets. The face, ears, tail and feet are also black. There is a light stripe running from the forehead to the tip of the muzzle.

DISTRIBUTION Brunei, Cambodia, Indonesia (Java, Kalimantan, Sumatra), Laos, Malaysia (Peninsular Malaysia, Sabah, Sarawak), Myanmar, Singapore, Thailand and Vietnam. Also found in China and India.

HABITS AND HABITAT Nocturnal and strongly arboreal, this civet is usually found alone or occasionally in pairs. It is primarily frugivorous, although a variety of small animals are sometimes included in the diet. It is found in primary or tall secondary forests up to at least 1,200m.

NOTES The loud shrill call of this civet helps one locate this species in the high trees at night. There are a number of subspecies, one of which, the Javan *A. t. trilineata*, may be a distinct species, but more research is required before this can be confirmed.

Banded Linsang ▪ *Prionodon linsang* HB 35–45cm, T 30–42cm

DESCRIPTION A small, long-bodied carnivore with buffy to golden fur and bold dark brown to black spots, which form approximately five bands across the back. The sides and legs are spotted. The long tail is banded with about seven broad dark rings. Spots on the side of the neck form longitudinal lines. The head is narrow with a pointed muzzle. It has short legs and, unlike civets, retractile claws.

DISTRIBUTION Brunei, Indonesia (Java, Kalimantan, Sumatra), Malaysia (Peninsular Malaysia, Sabah, Sarawak), Myanmar and Thailand.

HABITS AND HABITAT Little is known about the ecology of this nocturnal species. Found in primary and secondary forests, forest edges and disturbed forests, sometimes near human inhabited areas, it is largely arboreal but will forage on the ground as well, for birds, small mammals, reptiles and other small animals. It has been found up to 2,400m.

NOTES The two species of Asian linsang were until recently considered to be in the Viverridae family, with civets, but are now considered to belong to a family of their own (Prionodontidae).

> **MONGOOSES**
> Mongooses are similar in form to civets but have more pointed muzzles and tapering tails.

Small Asian Mongoose ■ *Herpestes javanicus* HB 36–42cm, T 27–32cm

DESCRIPTION The Small Asian Mongoose (or Javan Mongoose) is the smallest of South-East Asia's mongoose species, and the females are considerably smaller than the males. Speckled brown to reddish fur overall, with the head often especially reddish. Muzzle pointed, with a light brown to pinkish bare nose. Ears are small and rounded. Legs are relatively short, with small feet, and the tail is somewhat bushy and long.

DISTRIBUTION Cambodia, Indonesia (Java, Sumatra), Laos, Malaysia (Peninsular Malaysia), Myanmar, Thailand and Vietnam. Also found in Afghanistan, Bangladesh, Bhutan, China, India, Nepal and Pakistan. It has been introduced to a number of countries outside Asia.

HABITS AND HABITAT Found in a variety of habitats, especially in well-watered, naturally open forests and grasslands. It appears to prefer edge habitat in most areas and can be found in disturbed forests and scrubland, often close to human-inhabited areas. Like all Asian mongoose species, it is terrestrial and very rarely climbs trees. Largely diurnal, though occasionally active at night, hunting birds, rodents, reptiles, amphibians and other small animals.

NOTES Can sometimes be studied by the quiet observer, as it frequents open areas and forest edges often near human settlement, darting in and out of cover.

Collared Mongoose

■ *Herpestes semitorquatus*
HB 40–46cm, T 26–30cm

DESCRIPTION It has a reddish-brown coat with fine yellow markings on its back. Its throat is buff-orange and the lower parts of its legs are blackish brown. Sometimes bright orange coat, inviting confusion with Malay Weasel *Mustela nudipes*.

DISTRIBUTION Brunei, Indonesia (Kalimantan, Sumatra) and Malaysia (Sabah, Sarawak).

HABITS AND HABITAT The ecology of the Collared Mongoose is poorly known. It is thought to be found in a variety of habitats including tall and secondary forests, and in disturbed areas. It is mainly terrestrial and diurnal, and probably also active at night. Its diet includes small animals. Further studies are needed to determine its distribution and general life history.

Short-tailed Mongoose

■ *Herpestes brachyurus*
HB 38–45cm, T 20–25cm

DESCRIPTION The coat is blackish brown, with orange speckling that is obvious only at close range, and a pale brown chin and throat. The head and tail are paler than the rest of the body.

DISTRIBUTION Brunei, Indonesia (Kalimantan, Sumatra), Malaysia and Philippines (Palawan and the Calamian Islands).

HABITS AND HABITAT Like many small carnivores in the region, little is known of its ecology, though is thought to be found near rivers, in lowland primary and secondary forest and in plantations. It is mainly diurnal and terrestrial, with a diet that includes small animals and arthropods.

Tiger ▪ *Panthera tigris* HB 1.7–2.3m, T 0.95–1.15m

DESCRIPTION Unmistakable, with its large size and dark stripes on a deep orange coat. It has a pale underside and a ringed tail.

DISTRIBUTION Cambodia, Indonesia (Sumatra), Laos, Malaysia (Peninsular Malaysia), Myanmar, Thailand and Vietnam. Also found in Bangladesh, Bhutan, China, India, Nepal and Russia. In South-East Asia, extinct in Bali, Java and Singapore.

HABITS AND HABITAT Found in a variety of habitat types, from lower montane forest to riverine woodlands and peat swamps. Preys mainly on deer and wild pig, but also opportunistically feeds on a variety of other species, including ungulates much larger than itself. Generally solitary.

NOTES The Tiger's stripe patterns are like human fingerprints, and are used by researchers to identify individuals.

Leopard ▪ *Panthera pardus* HB 1–1.3m, T 0.8–1m

DESCRIPTION The Leopard is a large cat that occurs in two colour phases. The spotted form has black rosette spots on a yellowish-brown coat, and the melanistic form (often called the 'panther') has less obvious black rosette spots on a black coat, giving it an appearance of being an all-black cat, as the rosettes are only obvious in good light. The dark phase is more common in southern Thailand and Peninsular Malaysia. Nine subspecies are currently recognised globally.

DISTRIBUTION Cambodia, Indonesia (Java), Laos, Malaysia (Peninsular Malaysia), Myanmar, Thailand and Vietnam. A very widespread species, ranging throughout Africa and Central Asia to the Russian Far East.

HABITS AND HABITAT Found in all habitat types, Leopards have a very variable diet, taking a wider range of prey than any other cat. Frequently rests in trees.

Sunda Clouded Leopard ▪ *Neofelis diardi* HB 61–106cm, T 55–91cm

DESCRIPTION Irregular cloud-shaped markings on a greyish-yellow coat. It has large, black ovals on its underbelly and limbs and there are two dark bars on the back of its neck. Long, thickly furred tail. Proportionately, it has the longest canine teeth of any living cat.

DISTRIBUTION Brunei, Indonesia (Kalimantan, Sumatra) and Malaysia (Sabah, Sarawak).

HABITS AND HABITAT Primarily nocturnal, with crepuscular activity peaks. Highly arboreal, well adapted to climbing and creeping in the trees with its stout legs and broad paws. Forest-dependent, but it is found, perhaps at lower density, in logged forest. Preys on a wide variety of species, ranging from deer, pigs, primates and other mammals to fish.

NOTES This was considered a subspecies of the Clouded Leopard (*N. nebulosa*) until research in 2006 determined that it is a distinct species. It is Borneo's largest cat.

Marbled Cat ■ *Pardofelis marmorata* HB 45–53cm, T 47–55cm

DESCRIPTION This cat has thick fur with a complex marbled pattern of dark splotches and black lines on its back and stripes on its head. It has a very long thick tail.

DISTRIBUTION Brunei, Cambodia, Indonesia (Kalimantan, Sumatra), Laos, Malaysia (Peninsular Malaysia, Sabah, Sarawak), Myanmar, Thailand and Vietnam. Also found in Bhutan, China, India and Nepal.

HABITS AND HABITAT Primarily forest-dependent. Preys on small animals including rodents.

NOTES Studies show that the Marbled Cat is very closely related to the big cats, possibly similar to big cat ancestors 10 million years ago, but may have diminished in size recently due to competition.

Asian Golden Cat ▪ *Catopuma temminckii* HB 76–84cm, T 43–50cm

DESCRIPTION Coat varies from golden brown to tawny brown to greyish or black. Occasionally spotted. Black and white stripes on sides and front of head.

DISTRIBUTION Cambodia, Indonesia (Sumatra), Laos, Malaysia (Peninsular Malaysia), Myanmar, Thailand and Vietnam. Also found in Bangladesh, Bhutan, China, India and Nepal.

HABITS AND HABITAT Found in various forest habitats at a wide range of altitudes. Not primarily nocturnal, as previously thought. Mainly terrestrial but can climb trees.

NOTES On Borneo, the species is replaced by the closely similar Bay Cat *Pardofelis badia*.

Flat-headed Cat ■ *Prionailurus planiceps* HB 44–51cm, T 13–17cm

DESCRIPTION Narrow, flattened head with small ears. Semi-webbed toes. Greyish-brown coat with fine black speckling. Its chin and chest is white and it has faint pale and dark stripes on the sides of its face and forehead.

DISTRIBUTION Brunei, Indonesia (Kalimantan, Sumatra), Malaysia (Peninsular Malaysia, Sabah, Sarawak), and Thailand.

HABITS AND HABITAT Nocturnal and terrestrial, and found mainly in tall lowland forests, preferring areas close to streams. It is semi-aquatic, and its main diet is probably fish.

Leopard Cat ■ *Prionailurus bengalensis* HB 40–55cm, T 23–29cm

DESCRIPTION This is a small, lean cat. It has black spots on a reddish-orange or yellowish-buff coat, and the size and pattern of the spots can vary between individuals. Spots may be rounded or elongated and often almost join to look like stripes on its back. It is often confused with the larger Fishing Cat (p. 87).

DISTRIBUTION Brunei, Cambodia, Indonesia (Java, Kalimantan, Sumatra), Laos, Malaysia (Peninsular Malaysia, Sabah, Sarawak), Myanmar, Philippines, Singapore, Thailand and Vietnam. Also found in Afghanistan, Bangladesh, Bhutan, China, Hong Kong, India, Japan (Nansei-shoto), North and South Korea, Nepal, Pakistan, Russia and Taiwan.

HABITS AND HABITAT Relatively common, widespread in variety of habitats. Common in secondary forest and also in agricultural plantations. Preys mainly on small mammals. Nocturnal and mainly terrestrial, though it can climb small trees and is also a good swimmer.

Fishing Cat ■ *Prionailurus viverrinus* HB 72–78cm, T 25–29cm

DESCRIPTION A medium-large cat with light grey or olive-brown fur. It has black spots on its head and neck, small spots in rows on its flanks and back and a paler underside. It has partially webbed feet and a short tail.

DISTRIBUTION Cambodia, Indonesia (Java), Myanmar, Thailand and Vietnam. Presence in Laos, Peninsular Malaysia and Sumatra uncertain. Also found in Bangladesh, Bhutan, India, Nepal and Sri Lanka. Possibly extinct in Pakistan.

HABITS AND HABITAT Swamps, marshy areas, oxbow lakes, mangroves. Widely distributed but highly localised. At home in the water, it feeds mainly on fish, crabs and molluscs.

CETACEANS

Whales, dolphins and porpoises are cetaceans. Cetaceans are broadly split into two groups: the large baleen whales such as the Blue Whale (*Balaenoptera musculus*), and the toothed whales, such as the Sperm Whale (*Physeter macrocephalus*), along with all dolphins and porpoises.

Pantropical Spotted Dolphin ■ *Stenella attenuata* TL up to 2.6m

DESCRIPTION The Pantropical Spotted Dolphin is dark grey with a paler underside, usually heavily spotted. Slender elongated body with a long narrow beak, tipped with white. A dark stripe runs from beak to flipper. Prominent tall dorsal fin.

DISTRIBUTION Cambodia, Indonesia, Malaysia, Myanmar, Philippines, Singapore, Thailand and Vietnam. Presence in Brunei uncertain. Inhabits tropical, equatorial and southern subtropical water bodies worldwide. Most abundant near the equator.

HABITS AND HABITAT Off shore, spotted dolphins feed largely on small fish, squid and crustaceans. In some areas, flying fish are also important prey. The diet of coastal populations is poorly known, but is thought to consist mainly of larger fishes, perhaps mainly bottom-living species. Known for their impressive high leaps into the air.

NOTES This species is often associated with schools of tuna, and it has therefore been heavily impacted in the past by accidental killing in nets. Some deliberate hunting occurs in the region, including hand-harpoon fisheries in the Philippines.

Spinner Dolphin ■ *Stenella longirostris* TL 1.3–2.3m

DESCRIPTION Three-part colour pattern, dark on top, lighter grey on the sides and pale underparts. Long slender beak, with the upper jaw dark grey and the lower jaw cream. Dark stripe from eye to flipper. Gently sloping melon and a prominent dorsal fin.

DISTRIBUTION Brunei, Cambodia, Indonesia, Malaysia, Myanmar, Philippines, Singapore, Thailand and Vietnam. Found in tropical and subtropical waters worldwide. Four subspecies are recognised. In South-East Asia the Dwarf Spinner Dolphin (*S. l. roseiventris*) is distributed in shallow waters of inner South-East Asia, including the Gulf of Thailand, the Timor and Arafura Seas off northern Australia, and other similar shallow waters off Indonesia and Malaysia. It is replaced in deeper and outer waters by the larger pelagic subspecies *S. l. longirostris*.

HABITS AND HABITAT In most tropical waters, nearly all records of Spinner Dolphins are associated with inshore waters, islands or banks, although sometimes in very large numbers hundreds of kilometres from the nearest land. The Dwarf Spinner Dolphin in South-East Asian waters apparently inhabits shallow coral-reef habitat. Known for its incredibly high, spinning leaps. Often found in close association with Pantropical Spotted Dolphin (p. 88), Yellowfin Tuna (*Thunnus albacares*) and birds of several species.

NOTES Throughout their range, Spinner Dolphins are taken as by-catch in purse-seine, gillnet and trawl fisheries, and some populations have been reduced by more than half.

Irrawaddy Dolphin ▪ *Orcaella brevirostris* TL 2–2.8m

DESCRIPTION Grey to light grey, underparts paler. A very small dorsal fin behind the middle of the back. A high melon, rounded head and no beak. Large, rounded flippers.

DISTRIBUTION Brunei, Cambodia, Indonesia, Laos, Malaysia, Myanmar, Philippines, Singapore, Thailand and Vietnam. Also found in Bangladesh and India.

HABITS AND HABITAT Mainly found in shallow coastal waters, at brackish river mouths, near mangroves and in some major river systems, sometimes entering tributary rivers and lakes. Freshwater subpopulations are found in the Irrawaddy (up to 1,400km upstream) in Myanmar, the Mahakam (up to 560km upstream) in Indonesia, and the Mekong (up to 690km upstream) in Cambodia, Laos and Vietnam. Rarely leaps, and is quite quiet by nature.

NOTES The Irrawaddy Dolphin is threatened largely by entanglement in fishing gear, collisions with boats and habitat degradation. Capture for aquarium display is also a threat. More research and conservation efforts are urgently required.

False Killer Whale ■ *Pseudorca crassidens* TL up to 6m

DESCRIPTION The False Killer Whale, like all dolphins and porpoises, is a toothed whale. Uniformly dark except for paler areas on the throat and chest. Long slender body with a slender rounded head, with no beak. In adult males, the melon overhangs the lower jaw. Prominent dorsal fin and uniquely obvious elbows in the fins.

DISTRIBUTION Brunei, Cambodia, Indonesia, Malaysia, Myanmar, Philippines, Singapore, Thailand and Vietnam. Found in tropical and temperate waters worldwide.

HABITS AND HABITAT Usually found in relatively deep, offshore tropical and subtropical warm waters. Occasionally found in shallow and higher-latitude waters. Preys primarily on fish and cephalopods, but has been known to attack small cetaceans.

NOTES Normally encountered far off shore. They are suspected to be vulnerable to loud anthropogenic sounds, such as those generated by navy sonar and seismic exploration.

Melon-headed Whale ■ *Peponocephala electra* TL 2.2–2.6m

DESCRIPTION Dark grey to black, with a darker dorsal cape and facial markings. Underparts grey to white. Slim pointed head with no beak. Light grey or white lips. Large falcate fin.

DISTRIBUTION Brunei, Cambodia, Indonesia, Malaysia, Myanmar, Philippines, Singapore, Thailand and Vietnam. Pantropical distribution.

HABITS AND HABITAT Found in deep tropical and subtropical waters worldwide. Rarely ventures close to shore, except where water is deep. Sometimes found in groups of several hundred. Feeds largely on fish, squid and some crustaceans.

NOTES Sometimes travels with Fraser's Dolphins (*Lagenodelphis hosei*).

Dugong ■ *Dugong dugon* TL 2.5–3.3m

DESCRIPTION Dugongs are closely related to the manatees (*Trichechus* spp.) of America and Africa, looking fairly similar except that manatees have a round tail fluke with a single lobe and a divided upper lip. Dugongs are grey-brown in colour, with a long fusiform body, no dorsal fin, and whale-like tail flukes. A striking feature is the fleshy oral disk, an expanded region between the mouth and nose, which is covered with vibrissae. The location of the nostrils at the tip of the snout enables dugongs to breathe discreetly with only their nostrils out of the water. Dugongs have axillary mammary glands (teats) located under each flipper. Tusks erupt in adult males and a few very old females, but do not extend beyond the premaxilla. Weighs up to 500kg.

DISTRIBUTION Brunei, Cambodia, Indonesia, Malaysia, Myanmar, Philippines, Singapore, Thailand and Vietnam. Also found in tropical and subtropical coastal waters of more than 40 other countries.

HABITS AND HABITAT Usually found in small groups, but can be found in large herds in some parts of its range. The Dugong, a seagrass specialist, is the world's only herbivorous mammal that is strictly marine. Tides can restrict its foraging on intertidal seagrass meadows on a daily basis.

NOTES The Dugong makes bird-like chirps that are inaudible above water. It is the only surviving member of the family Dugongidae, and very likely one of the most threatened marine mammals in South-East Asia, due to hunting, entanglement in fishing gear, collisions with boats and habitat destruction.

Asian Elephant ■ *Elephas maximus* SH 1.5–3m, HB 3–6m, T 1–1.5m

DESCRIPTION Greyish-brown thick and wrinkly skin. Not all elephants have tusks; some adult males have long tusks reaching up to 2m, but females and younger males have tushes, which are shorter tusks that are usually not visible. Its back is rounded and sloped, making its crown the highest point of its body. Asian Elephants have smaller ears than African elephants (*Loxodonta* spp.).

DISTRIBUTION Cambodia, Indonesia (Kalimantan, Sumatra), Laos, Malaysia (Peninsular Malaysia, Sabah), Myanmar, Thailand and Vietnam. Also found in Bangladesh, Bhutan, China, India, Nepal and Sri Lanka. Extinct in Pakistan.

HABITS AND HABITAT A highly social animal, living in herds of related females and juveniles, led by a matriarch. Males leave their herds when they mature at about 6–7 years of age and become predominantly solitary, seeking females for mating purposes only. An elephant can consume up to 150kg of vegetation daily. It eats mainly grasses but also fruit, bark and other plants. It is an excellent swimmer. Elephants practise allomothering, where females in the herd care for and protect all the young in the herd as they would their own.

■ ELEPHANT ■

ABOVE AND BELOW, RIGHT: *Pygmy Elephant*

NOTES The elephants in the Malaysian state of Sabah are sometimes considered a distinct subspecies, the Bornean Elephant, also called the Pygmy Elephant because of its smaller size. This is still subject to debate, however, and some believe that these elephants, which have a highly limited distribution, are not native, and may actually be descendants of an introduced population. A good place to view them is along the Kinabatangan River, by boat.

Asian Tapir ▪ *Tapirus indicus* SH 0.9–1.05m, HB 2–2.4m, T 5–10cm

DESCRIPTION The closest relatives of the tapirs are horses and rhinoceroses. There are four tapir species globally but only one occurs in Asia. The Asian Tapir is the largest of the tapirs, with a stocky build and very distinctive black and white colouring. The front part of the body, including the head and forelegs, and the hind legs, are black. The remainder of the body is white. Its elongated nose and upper lip form a prominent prehensile proboscis, an important adaptation that the tapir uses to grasp vegetation. Infants are born dark grey with short, horizontal white stripes and spots in rows.

HABITS AND HABITAT Found in primary and secondary forest, both montane and lowland. While it seems to prefer intact primary rainforest, it is also found in secondary growth and degraded habitat as well. Often prefers streams and rivers. Largely solitary by nature and mainly nocturnal. Eats a wide variety of plant matter.

DISTRIBUTION Indonesia (Sumatra), Malaysia (Peninsular Malaysia), Myanmar and Thailand.

NOTES At a glance, the black and white colouration may seem very conspicuous, but this disruptive patterning actually helps break up its body outline in shady and moonlit forests, just like the tiger's striped coat.

Sumatran Rhinoceros ■ *Dicerorhinus sumatrensis*

SH 1.2–1.3m, HB 2.4–2.6m, T 35–70cm

DESCRIPTION The Sumatran Rhinoceros is dark brownish grey with a large heavy body and thick skin. One fold of skin crosses the back behind the shoulders. Sparse hair covers the body, especially in young animals. Three toes on each foot. Two horns, with the front horn longer and thinner than the much smaller rear horn, which is sometimes barely visible. This is the smallest of the rhinos.

DISTRIBUTION Indonesia (Kalimantan, Sumatra), Malaysia (Peninsular Malaysia, Sabah, Sarawak) and Myanmar (possibly extinct). Extinct in Brunei, Cambodia, Laos, Thailand and Vietnam. Also extinct in Bangladesh, Bhutan and India. Three subspecies: *D. s. lasiotis* (probably extinct), *D. s. sumatrensis* and *D. s. harrissoni*.

HABITS AND HABITAT The Sumatran Rhinoceros is extremely shy, and is generally solitary except for mating pairs and mothers with young. It occurs from sea level to over 2,500m, inhabiting tropical rainforest and montane moss forest, and occasionally at forest margins and in secondary forest. Found mainly in hilly areas near water sources, spending the hotter parts of the day resting, often in wallows of mud.

NOTES The two principal threats are poaching for the horns and the resulting reduced population viability. The horns are believed to have medicinal properties, and despite trade in these being illegal, poaching continues, leaving the total population at an estimated 275 or fewer. It is of paramount importance that efforts to save this species from extinction are stepped up in effectiveness and scale.

Javan Rhinoceros ■ *Rhinoceros sondaicus* SH 1.6–1.8m, HB 3–3.2m, T 70cm

DESCRIPTION Large and heavy with thick dark grey skin, with three folds of skin across the back. A single horn at the tip of the snout, often inconspicuous in females.

DISTRIBUTION Indonesia (Java). Extinct in Cambodia, Indonesia (Sumatra), Laos, Malaysia (Peninsular Malaysia), Myanmar, Thailand and Vietnam. Also extinct in Bangladesh, China and India. Originally three recognised subspecies: *R. s. sondaicus*, *R. s. annamiticus* and *R. s. inermis* (the latter two extinct).

HABITS AND HABITAT This is a lowland species that typically occurs up to 600m, but has been recorded above 1,000m. Formerly occurred in more open mixed forest and grassland and on high mountains. Because of its extreme rarity, little is known about its preferred habitat.

NOTES Poaching for the horn has pushed the Javan Rhinoceros to the brink of extinction. An estimated 40–60 animals live in the area on the western tip of Java in Ujung Kulon National Park, and nowhere else. Failure to protect this species in Vietnam, the last population outside of Java, led to its extinction there in 2011. Efforts to save this species from total extinction are needed urgently.

Eurasian Wild Pig ▪ *Sus scrofa* SH 60–80cm, HB 135–150cm, T 20–30cm

DESCRIPTION The colour of this species varies from reddish to blackish, with long black hairs on its upper back and neck, forming a mane. It has an elongated muzzle, with males having enlarged, protruding canines. Juveniles are dark brown with elongated white stripes along the body. It is similar to the Sunda Bearded Pig (p. 101), but is smaller and lacks the extensive beard.

DISTRIBUTION Cambodia, Indonesia, Laos, Malaysia (Peninsular Malaysia), Myanmar, Singapore, Thailand and Vietnam. The Eurasian Wild Pig has the largest range of all pigs, found in numerous countries worldwide including much of Europe, North Africa and mainland Asia.

HABITS AND HABITAT Found in a wide variety of habitats, from mature and secondary forests to disturbed areas and plantations. It is an omnivore, eating roots, tubers, fruit, seeds, other vegetation and animal matter encountered on the ground, such as eggs, nestlings and worms. Mainly active early in the day and late afternoon, but human disturbance can make them nocturnal. Lives in large herds of up to 20 individuals, though there have been instances of over 100 gathering.

NOTES At a global level, there are no major threats to the species. However, there are many threats at a more local level, principally hunting pressure, for food, for sport or in reprisal for crop damage, particularly in areas near human habitation.

Javan Warty Pig ▪ *Sus verrucosus* SH 70–90cm, HB 90–190cm

DESCRIPTION Reddish in colour, although sometimes appearing blackish. Underparts are white or yellowish. Large head, with large ears, and in males three pairs of facial 'warts', lacking in females. Males are up to twice as large as females. Both sexes have a long mane, often a lighter orange-brown colour, on top of the head and along the spine to the rump. Long thin legs and a long tail with a tuft of hair at the end. Two subspecies are recognised. In the field, they can appear similar to Eurasian Wild Pig (p. 99).

DISTRIBUTION This species is endemic to Indonesia, where it was historically found on Java, Madura Island (extinct) and Bawean Island. It now remains in only small pockets of fragmented and rapidly shrinking habitat – on Java it now survives in at least 10 separate, isolated areas.

HABITS AND HABITAT Occurs in cultivated areas and teak plantations, as well as in remaining stands of forest. It appears to thrive in mosaics of forest–teak plantations, scrub and open grasslands, and seems to prefer secondary forests over primary forests. It is restricted to elevations below 800m and is often found in mangrove and swamp forests. Lives in small groups of 4–6 individuals.

NOTES This species is in trouble. Its decline is due to habitat fragmentation, hybridisation with Eurasian Wild Pig and intense hunting pressure, for food, for sport and to protect crops. This species is also (illegally) pitted against dogs for sport. Captive breeding programmes are under way to ensure that the Javan Warty Pig is not lost.

Sunda Bearded Pig ■ *Sus barbatus* SH 70–90cm, HB 120–150cm, T 17–25cm

DESCRIPTION Colour varies from blackish (in young animals) to grey, reddish brown or yellowish brown. Appearance is affected by the colour of mud the pig has been wallowing in. Large, long head with long thick bristles on snout. A fleshy protuberance on the sides of the snout above the mouth. Lower canines of males protrude. Hoof prints are rounded and symmetrical, with distinct dew toes.

DISTRIBUTION Brunei, Indonesia (Kalimantan, Sumatra), Malaysia (Peninsular Malaysia, Sabah, Sarawak) and Philippines (extreme south).

HABITS AND HABITAT Diurnal and nocturnal – largely nocturnal in areas with heavy hunting pressure. Most often found in tropical evergreen rainforest, but also in a wide variety of habitat types, ranging from beaches to upper montane forests. Large-scale population movements, over weeks or months, have often been recorded, reportedly linked to the availability of seasonal fruits, particularly mast-fruiting species, i.e. those with huge variation between years in fruit production.

NOTES Borneo represents the best place to view this species, although they may be seen with a great deal of luck in other parts of their range, such as in Endau Rompin National Park in Peninsular Malaysia.

> **CHEVROTAINS**
> The chevrotains are also known as mouse-deer, referring to their small size – though they are not deer.

Lesser Oriental Chevrotain ▪ *Tragulus kanchil*

SH 20–23cm, HB 40–55cm, T 6–9cm

DESCRIPTION The upperparts are reddish brown mixed with fine black fur, the centre of the nape being darker than the rest of the back, often appearing like a dark stripe. It has white underparts, with variable brown stripes in the middle and along the sides of its body. It has distinctive dark brown and white markings on its throat and upper chest, typically with a triangular white stripe in the middle, bordered by a dark brown triangle, with diagonal white stripes on the side, which usually join at the chin. Legs very slender. Males have visible protruding canines.

DISTRIBUTION Brunei, Cambodia, Indonesia, Laos, Malaysia (Peninsular Malaysia, Sabah, Sarawak), Myanmar, Singapore, Thailand and Vietnam. Presence in China uncertain.

HABITS AND HABITAT Lowland primary and secondary forest, as well as cultivated areas. It is usually solitary, and is active periodically during both night and day. Its diet comprises shoots, young leaves, fallen fruit and fungi.

Greater Oriental Chevrotain ■ *Tragulus napu*
SH 30–35cm, HB 52–57cm, T 6–10cm

DESCRIPTION This species has coarsely mottled orange-buff, grey-buff and blackish upperparts, which are darker in the midline and paler along the sides of its body. Often, it has a darker nape patch. The intensity of the colouration varies between individuals. It has white underparts, usually without belly stripes. It has a pattern of brown and white markings on the underside of its neck and upper chest, typically with a triangular white stripe in the centre bordered by dark brown stripes. It has two white stripes on each side, which appear as two separate white bars on the side of the neck when viewed in profile.

DISTRIBUTION Brunei, Indonesia (Kalimantan, Sumatra), Malaysia (Peninsular Malaysia, Sabah, Sarawak), Myanmar, Singapore and Thailand.

HABITS AND HABITAT Found in mainly tall and secondary forest. It is mainly nocturnal but can be active during the day as well. Its diet includes leaf shoots, fallen fruit and other vegetation.

NOTES The Greater Oriental Chevrotain was thought to be extinct in Singapore until it was rediscovered in 2008 on Pulau Ubin, a small island off the northeastern corner of mainland Singapore.

Balabac Chevrotain ▪ *Tragulus nigricans* SH 18cm, HB 40–50cm, T 8cm

DESCRIPTION Upperparts washed with black, mottled with orange, with three narrow white bars on the throat and chest, starting from a white patch under the chin. Its nose bridge and forehead are dark brown, leading to a dark crown. Like other chevrotains, it is small, with very slender legs.

DISTRIBUTION Philippines (Balabac, Bugsuc and Ramos Islands). Its presence in Malaysia is uncertain, making it endemic to the Philippines until confirmed otherwise.

HABITS AND HABITAT Not much is known about this species, but it is known to occur in primary and secondary lowland forest and shrubland, and it may frequent mangroves and more open areas to forage.

NOTES The chevrotains on the small Malaysian island of Pulau Banggi, located midway between Balabac and the Bornean mainland, might belong to this species – but further studies are required.

Red Muntjac ■ *Muntiacus muntjak* SH 50–55cm, HB 90–110cm, T 17–19cm

DESCRIPTION A small deer with reddish-brown to paler reddish-yellow coat, generally darker along the midline, with paler underparts. The underside of the tail is white. Males have small, thick antlers with a small spike at the base and the pedicels have very obvious black lines, which continue onto the antlers. Females have a stiff tuft of hair on the top of the head instead of antlers and pedicels. Juveniles have white spots, which they lose as they mature.

DISTRIBUTION Brunei, Cambodia, Indonesia (Java, Kalimantan, Sumatra), Laos, Malaysia (Peninsular Malaysia, Sabah, Sarawak), Myanmar, Thailand and Vietnam. Extinct in Singapore. Also found in Bangladesh, Bhutan, China, Hong Kong, India, Nepal, Pakistan and Sri Lanka.

HABITS AND HABITAT Found in a variety of habitats, from tropical to dry dipterocarp, lowland and hill forests. It mainly eats leaves, shoots and fallen fruit. Primarily nocturnal, although in sites with less hunting and other human disturbance they are also active during the day.

NOTES Both males and females emit an alarm call that sounds like a bark, which gives this species its other common name, the Common Barking Deer.

Sambar ▪ *Rusa unicolor* SH 140–160cm, HB 150–200cm, T 21–28cm

DESCRIPTION A large-bodied deer. Dark to greyish brown, darker along the midline. Adult males have three tines to each antler, and long, coarse neck hair. The young may have light spots.

DISTRIBUTION Brunei, Cambodia, Indonesia (Kalimantan, Sumatra and some smaller islands), Laos, Malaysia (Peninsular Malaysia, Sabah, Sarawak), Myanmar, Thailand and Vietnam. Also found in Bangladesh, Bhutan, China, India, Nepal, Sri Lanka and Taiwan.

HABITS AND HABITAT Mainly nocturnal. Eats grasses, herbs, shrubs, leaves. Frequents salt licks. Usually solitary and nocturnal, possibly a consequence of severe hunting pressure. Very much declined in many areas due to to poaching.

NOTES Easily viewed in certain protected areas in Thailand, such as Khao Yai National Park, Thap Lan National Park and Phu Khieo Wildlife Sanctuary.

Eld's Deer ▪ *Rucervus eldii* SH 120–130cm, HB 150–170cm, T 22–25cm

DESCRIPTION Brown with white belly. The adult male's antlers have a prominent brow tine that forms a continuous curve with the main branch, which has a few small tines at its tip. The bow-shaped antlers grow outwards and then inwards, rather than just upwards.

DISTRIBUTION Cambodia, Laos and Myanmar. Possibly extinct in Thailand and Vietnam. Also found in China and India.

HABITS AND HABITAT Found in lowland swamps, dry dipterocarp and grasslands. Diet of grass, browse, fallen fruit and flowers. Forms large herds where not hunted. Due largely to poaching, this species has undergone severe population declines.

MAIN PICTURE: *Male.* INSET: *Female with fawn*

Hog Deer ■ *Axis porcinus* SH 65–72cm, HB 140–150cm, T 17–21cm

DESCRIPTION Similar to Sambar (p. 106), but smaller, with shorter legs. Light brown fur. Slender antlers on males. Young are heavily spotted. Females may retain spots.

DISTRIBUTION Cambodia, Myanmar, and reintroduced in Thailand. Also found in Bangladesh, Bhutan, India, Nepal and Pakistan. Presence in Laos and Vietnam uncertain. Extinct in China.

HABITS AND HABITAT Seasonally inundated (natural flooding) lowland grasslands. Mainly feeds on grasses.

NOTES Efforts to reintroduce the species in Thailand are ongoing. It has been extirpated mainly because of over-hunting and habitat loss. Its main habitat is prime rice growing land – rice is a grass that grows best under seasonal inundation. So it remains only in small isolated areas from which it is easily hunted out.

Calamian Deer ■ *Axis calamianensis* SH 60–100cm, HB 100–175cm, T 12–38cm

DESCRIPTION Heavy-bodied, though fairly small. It is tawny-brown with darker legs and underparts. It has subtle white markings around its muzzle, and the underside of the tail is also white. Males have three-pronged antlers.

DISTRIBUTION Philippines. Endemic to the Calamian islands of the Palawan Faunal Region.

HABITS AND HABITAT Found in grasslands, open woodlands and secondary forest. It is diurnal, and eats mainly leaves. It lives in small herds, generally between 7 and 14 individuals, but groups of up to 27 have been recorded. In heavily hunted areas, groups tend to be smaller.

> **Cattle, Buffalo, Goats and Sheep**
> Cattle, buffalo, goats and sheep belong to the family Bovidae, which also includes antelopes. One of the defining characteristics of this family is the presence of unbranched horns, which are never shed and continue to grow as the animal ages.

Takin ▪ *Budorcas taxicolor* SH 0.7–1.4m, HB 1–1.4m, T 7–12cm

DESCRIPTION The Takin has long and shaggy hair, varying in colour from dark brown to a light golden brown. Females and young are often greyer than males. it is a thick-bodied animal with an arched back, thick neck, thick legs and an outwardly curved face. Horns arise from the middle of the forehead, turning outwards and then curving backwards. Females and juveniles have straighter horns than males.

DISTRIBUTION Myanmar. Also found in Bhutan, China and India.

HABITS AND HABITAT Found in hill forests, feeding in open areas and sheltering in forests. In summer, feeds in alpine meadows up to 4,000m, and in winter, in valleys and forests to as low as 1,000m. Eats a variety of grasses, bamboo shoots, and leaves of shrubs and trees. Mostly active in early morning and late afternoon. Often in small herds of 20–30, but occasionally up to 300. Older males are solitary for much of the year.

NOTES Four subspecies are recognised, with only *B. t. taxicolor* found in South-East Asia, in northern Myanmar.

▪ CATTLE, BUFFALO, GOATS AND SHEEP ▪

Banteng ▪ *Bos javanicus* SH 1.5–1.7m, HB 1.9–2.25m, T 65–70cm

DESCRIPTION Males are dark brown, often black, while females and immature males are bright rufous brown. Both sexes have a white band across the muzzle, white buttocks and white 'stockings' on the lower parts of the legs. Mature females are smaller than mature males. Horns curve outwards and forward, with a horny patch of skin between the horns.

DISTRIBUTION Cambodia, Indonesia (Bali, Java, Kalimantan), Laos, Malaysia (Peninsular Malaysia, Sabah, Sarawak), Myanmar, Thailand and Vietnam. Extinct in Brunei. Also possibly found in southern China. Extinct in Bangladesh and India.

HABITS AND HABITAT Prefers open flat or undulating terrain with dry deciduous forests and open grassland mosaics over closed evergreen forests, although in some areas it occupies secondary forest formations resulting from logging and fires. Due to human pressure, Banteng increasingly use less preferred habitat, and are somewhat adaptable. Feeding grounds tend to be near permanent water supplies.

NOTES Banteng are largely diurnal, but hunting pressure has resulted in most populations adapting to a nocturnal existence. The largest remaining natural populations are in Indonesia (Java) and Thailand.

Gaur ▪ *Bos gaurus* SH 1.7–1.85m, HB 2.5–3m, T 70–105cm

DESCRIPTION Massive. Both sexes are very dark brown, almost black, with whitish or yellowish 'stockings' on the lower parts of the legs. Adult males have a thick muscular ridge on the back. Horns curve outwards and upwards. Lacks the white buttocks of Banteng.

DISTRIBUTION Cambodia, Laos, Malaysia (Peninsular Malaysia), Myanmar, Thailand and Vietnam. Also found in Bangladesh, Bhutan, China, India and Nepal.

HABITS AND HABITAT Forested areas, feeding on grasslands. Mainly nocturnal, and favours salt licks.

NOTES Heavily hunted in much of its range. Several protected areas in Thailand have growing populations, including Khao Yai National Park and Huai Kha Khaeng Wildlife Sanctuary.

Wild Water Buffalo ▪ *Bubalus arnee* SH 1.6–1.9m, HB 2.4–2.8m, T 60–85cm

DESCRIPTION Larger than Domestic Water Buffalo (*Bubalus bubalis*), with broader and wider-spread horns, the broadest of any living bovid.

DISTRIBUTION Cambodia, Myanmar and Thailand. Possibly extinct in Vietnam. Extinct in Laos. Also found in Bangladesh, Bhutan, India and Nepal. Possibly extinct in Sri Lanka.

HABITS AND HABITAT Prefers grasslands and open forests, near water. Frequently wallows in mud and pools. Lives in small herds.

NOTES Fewer than 4,000 remain, with populations highly fragmented and threatened by hunting, habitat loss and interbreeding with Domestic Water Buffalo.

Tamaraw ▪ *Bubalus mindorensis* SH 1–1.05m, HB 2.2m, T 60cm

DESCRIPTION A small buffalo, very dark brown in colour, with a white patch on the throat and sometimes white 'stockings' on the lower legs. Both sexes have horns that point backwards, and not in a broad arc as in the Domestic Water Buffalo (*Bubalus bubalis*). Males have larger horns than females.

DISTRIBUTION Philippines. Endemic to the island of Mindoro.

HABITS AND HABITAT Once widespread across Mindoro, in a range of habitats from sea level to mountainous areas, in marshes, bamboo forests, mixed forests and grasslands, this highly threatened species is now confined to two or three areas, in rough terrain in remote inaccessible areas. Mixed grassland and forest mosaics are most likely the preferred habitat. Largely solitary or in female–offspring pairs. Now extremely rare due to overhunting.

NOTES Because of hunting pressure, this formerly diurnal species has become nocturnal.

Sumatran Serow ■ *Capricornis sumatraensis*

SH 85–94cm, HB 140–155cm, T 11–16cm

DESCRIPTION Black upper- and underparts. Hairs do not have white bases except those on the mane and along the back either side of black dorsal stripe. The mane varies from mostly white, or golden buffy-white, to black with only a few white hairs. Short white jaw streaks quickly becoming red then black. Long legs black, with distinct (varying) reddish tones towards the hoofs, occasionally with white hairs. There is a large open gland in front of each eye. The horns in both sexes curve back slightly from the forehead, with horizontal ridges.

DISTRIBUTION Indonesia (Sumatra), Malaysia (Peninsular Malaysia) and possibly in peninsular Thailand.

HABITS AND HABITAT This serow is often found on steep mountain slopes between 200 and 3,000m, covered by both primary and secondary forests. It is also often found on forested limestone karsts. Regular latrines are used, often under overhanging rocks or cliff faces. Solitary, but also recorded in small groups of up to seven.

NOTES Habitat loss, including limestone and quartz-ridge quarrying, as well as hunting, are serious threats.

Burmese Red Serow ■ *Capricornis rubidus*

SH 85–95cm, HB 140–155cm, T 11–16cm

DESCRIPTION Red-brown, with more red on the neck and flanks, with hairs having black bases. The underside is white. There is a black dorsal line and a dark red mane, which is shorter than in other serow species, and a short tail. Nose, jaw and throat patch are white, creamy red or red. Long ears and a large open gland in front of each eye. Horns in both sexes curve back slightly from the forehead, with horizontal ridges.

DISTRIBUTION Myanmar.

HABITS AND HABITAT Tropical and subtropical hill and montane forests, including rugged limestone hills. Serow tend to be somewhat solitary, except females with young.

NOTES The Burmese Red Serow has only recently been split from the red serow species occurring in Assam, India, whose taxonomic status is currently uncertain.

Saola ▪ *Pseudoryx nghetinhensis* SH 80–90cm, HB 150cm, T 23cm

DESCRIPTION Overall deep chestnut brown, varying from rich reddish brown to almost black. The anal area and inner flanks are white. A thin black stripe runs along the spine from between the shoulders to the top of the tail. A white horizontal stripe runs across the rump, with a white band across the tail. The legs are darker than the main body and have two white spots above the hooves. The face is marked with white to buff patches, the most distinctive of which is a long, thin 'eyebrow' stripe above each eye. There is a variable pattern of spots and slashes from beneath the eye to under the jaw, while a single white spot may be present on the cheek. White lips, underside of chin and upper throat. Both sexes have long, slender horns that curve slightly backwards and reach 35–50cm long.

DISTRIBUTION Laos and Vietnam.

HABITS AND HABITAT Found in forested habitats in the Annamite mountains, in closed canopy, broadleaf evergreen forests, usually at 400–800m above sea level. It has been suggested that there are seasonal movements between elevations, and different forest types. Forest blocks smaller than 25km² and agricultural areas are not used, highlighting the need to preserve large blocks of tall forest. Probably largely solitary, though sometimes in groups of two or three, and perhaps up to six or seven. Natural predators potentially include Leopard *Panthera pardus*, Tiger *P. tigris* and Dhole *Cuon alpinus*.

NOTES The Saola represents one of the more amazing animal discoveries in recent times, with the first record of this species coming to the scientific world only in 1992. Hunting, often with dogs, and death in snares that are often set for other species, represent the greatest threats to its survival, followed closely by habitat loss. Probably numbering less than a few hundred, it is one of the most seriously threatened large mammals in the world.

Black Giant Squirrel ■ *Ratufa bicolor* HB 37–41cm, T 42–50cm

DESCRIPTION Squirrels are small to large-sized rodents. The Black Giant Squirrel is the largest squirrel in South-East Asia and quite variable in appearance. Upperparts, including the top of the head, are generally black, but can be brown or slightly reddish-tinged black. Underparts are pale cream or buff to orange, running down the front legs. The feet are blackish, as is the entire tail. The face is largely white to reddish with a black moustache-like stripe extending across the cheeks. One subspecies, *R. b. smithi*, is buff in colour from the nape, down the back and sometimes onto the tail, and has pale areas on front and hind limbs.

DISTRIBUTION Cambodia, Indonesia (Bali, Java, Sumatra), Laos, Malaysia (Peninsular Malaysia), Myanmar, Thailand and Vietnam. Also found in Bangladesh, Bhutan, China and Nepal.

HABITS AND HABITAT Diurnal and arboreal, occasionally venturing to forest floor to feed. Found in tropical and subtropical montane evergreen and dry deciduous forests, often in tall secondary forests, and in some parts of its range near human settlements. Can be quite common in areas with suitable habitat and low levels of hunting.

NOTES Although still fairly widespread, this species has an increasingly patchy distribution throughout its range, although possibly less so in Malaysia.

Cream-coloured Giant Squirrel ■ *Ratufa affinis*

HB 31–38cm, T 37–44cm

DESCRIPTION Large. Buff-brown to orange-brown, becoming darker in colour in the northern parts of its range. Animals on Borneo are much darker. Underparts are pale buff to whitish.

DISTRIBUTION Brunei, Indonesia (Kalimantan, Sumatra), Malaysia, (Peninsular Malaysia, Sabah, Sarawak), Singapore and Thailand. This species has not been seen in Singapore since 1995 and may be extirpated, due largely to habitat destruction.

HABITS AND HABITAT Diurnal and strictly arboreal, found in tall closed-canopy forests. It occurs in lowland and hilly areas, sometimes in selectively logged areas, but appears generally to avoid plantations.

NOTES This squirrel occurs in relatively low densities throughout its range, possibly because of competition for food with other arboreal vertebrates such as birds and primates. Loss of tall trees, as well as hunting for consumption, is a serious threat to this species.

Plantain Squirrel ■ *Callosciurus notatus* HB 17–22cm, T 16–21cm

DESCRIPTION A medium-sized squirrel with brownish upperparts and underparts reddish orange, varying from pale to dark. The tail is tipped with orange, which is more obvious in some individuals than others. Two stripes run down its sides, with a dark stripe next to the belly and a light stripe above that.

DISTRIBUTION Brunei, Indonesia (Java, Kalimantan, Sumatra), Malaysia (Peninsular Malaysia, Sabah, Sarawak), Singapore and Thailand. Also found on smaller islands within this range.

HABITS AND HABITAT Diurnal and arboreal, this squirrel is quite adaptable, found in a wide variety of habitats, including secondary forests, plantations, parks, gardens and along forest edge. Less common in primary forests. Found from lowland up to 1,500m. Its diet consists mostly of fruit and bark, as well as some insects.

NOTES As it is very adaptable, its range has expanded with human-related habitat alteration. It is not currently threatened, although in some areas it is heavily hunted for consumption.

Slender Squirrel ▪ *Sundasciurus tenuis* HB 11–16cm, T 12–13cm

DESCRIPTION Small, with slightly speckled brown-olive upperparts and light grey to whitish underparts. Slender tail, pale eye-rings, and a nose that appears slightly upturned.

DISTRIBUTION Brunei, Indonesia (Kalimantan, Sumatra and some smaller islands), Malaysia (Peninsular Malaysia, Sabah, Sarawak), Singapore and southern peninsular Thailand.

HABITS AND HABITAT Diurnal and arboreal, it is found in primary and secondary forests, in both lowlands and mountains, and in parks and gardens.

NOTES Similar to Low's Squirrel (p. 122), but has greyer underparts and a longer, more slender tail. Has adapted to city park life in parts of its range and can be quite easily observed in Singapore.

Low's Squirrel ■ *Sundasciurus lowii* HB 13–15cm, T 8–10cm

DESCRIPTION Brown to reddish brown, sometimes with slight speckles. The underside is buffy, sometimes with a reddish colour. Slight reddish eye-ring and a very bushy tail.

DISTRIBUTION Brunei, Indonesia (Kalimantan, Sumatra and a few smaller islands), Malaysia (Peninsular Malaysia, Sabah, Sarawak) and peninsular Thailand.

HABITS AND HABITAT Diurnal, found in small trees and sometimes seen foraging on the ground. This small squirrel is fond of secondary and disturbed forests, but occurs at relatively low densities, possibly due to competition for food from other tree-dwelling vertebrates, such as birds, primates and other squirrels. It is usually found below 900m, but on Borneo it occurs up to 1,400m.

Western Striped Squirrel ■ *Tamiops mcclellandii*

HB 11–12.5cm, T 11–14cm

DESCRIPTION Upperparts are mottled grey and brown with five dark stripes and four pale stripes running the length of the back, with the central stripes being the darkest. The pale stripes vary from white to cream or buff, with the outer pair wider and brighter than the inner pair. The outer pale stripes are continuous with white stripes on the cheeks. Underparts are pale buff to orangeish. White tufts on ears. Superficially resembles chipmunks (*Tamias* spp.) and is sometimes mistakenly referred to as such.

DISTRIBUTION Laos, Malaysia (Peninsular Malaysia), Myanmar, Thailand and Vietnam. Also found in Bhutan, China, India and Nepal.

HABITS AND HABITAT A wide array of habitats, including primary and secondary forests, scrub and degraded forests and gardens, especially with fruit trees and coconut palms. Often found in hilly or mountainous areas in the Sundaic part of its range, usually above 700m. In northern South-East Asia, it is common at lower elevations.

NOTES Further research is required, as the genus *Tamiops* is in need of taxonomic review and this species may represent a species complex (currently there are four species described). Species range limits remain poorly understood. This tiny squirrel very often feeds in the proximity of mixed bird flocks, possibly taking advantage of the extra eyes watching out for danger.

Prevost's Squirrel ■ *Callosciurus prevostii* HB 20–27cm, T 20–27cm

DESCRIPTION One of the most colourful squirrels in the region, with pelage differing greatly in various parts of the region. All forms have dark reddish or orange underparts. The mainland South-East Asia form has black upperparts with a white stripe on the flanks. The sides of the face are grey. There are a number of subspecies on Borneo, ranging from entirely black upperparts to grizzled olive-buff or grizzled brown, some with reddish shoulders or thighs, and tails ranging from black to grizzled brown or grey.

DISTRIBUTION Brunei, Indonesia (Kalimantan, Sumatra), Malaysia (Peninsular Malaysia, Sabah, Sarawak) and peninsular Thailand. It also occurs on many smaller islands throughout this range.

HABITS AND HABITAT Diurnal and arboreal, rarely venturing to the ground to forage or to cross gaps in the forest. It is found in lowland primary and secondary forests, but also uses oil-palm and coconut plantations that are adjacent to forests.

NOTES Habitat continues to be destroyed and fragmented, with much of the natural habitat of this species being replaced by plantations. In some parts of its range it is threatened by hunting for consumption and to be used as pets. More research on the impact of these threats is needed.

Pallas's Squirrel ■ *Callosciurus erythraeus* HB 20–26cm, T 19–25cm

DESCRIPTION Variable in colouration throughout the region. In most, upperparts
are agouti; brownish to greyish white. In some populations, sometimes with a black
stripe down the back. Underparts are reddish or reddish brown to grey-brown. In some
populations there is an agouti-coloured stripe running down the middle of the belly,
separating the reddish colouration into two stripes. In some populations, the entire body
is reddish, with underparts pale orange. The black dorsal stripe varies in width from one
population to another, or is absent.

DISTRIBUTION Cambodia, Laos, Malaysia (Peninsular Malaysia), Myanmar, Thailand and
Vietnam. Also found in Bangladesh, China, India and Taiwan.

HABITS AND HABITAT Diurnal and arboreal. Found in primary and secondary forests,
as well as in orchards and disturbed habitat. Often in hilly areas. Nests in tree-hollows in
mid-canopy.

Black Flying Squirrel ■ *Aeromys tephromelas* HB 33–43cm, T 41–47cm

DESCRIPTION A large dark grey to blackish flying squirrel with a dark face and a long dark tail. Some light speckles on the upperparts. Underparts are similar but paler.

DISTRIBUTION Brunei, Indonesia (Kalimantan, Sumatra), Malaysia (Peninsular Malaysia, Sabah, Sarawak) and southern Thailand.

HABITS AND HABITAT Like other flying squirrels, this species is nocturnal and arboreal. It appears to be quite adaptable and is found in primary forests and tall secondary forests, as well as in tree plantations and in gardens with tall trees. Shelters in hollows in trees. It is usually found in hilly areas.

NOTES Like the colugos (pp. 17–18), flying squirrels do not, strictly speaking, fly – they glide from one tree to another, using the patagium (a membrane on each side of the body joining fore and hind limbs) like a glider.

Indian Giant Flying Squirrel ▪ *Petaurista philippensis*
HB 40–49cm, T 40–55cm

DESCRIPTION Upperparts, gliding membrane and tail are grey-brown with long hairs on the back heavily frosted with white. Underparts light grey. Some geographic variation, with upperparts reddish, dark brown or dark grey, with frosting, and underparts pale orange to buff.

DISTRIBUTION Cambodia, Laos, Myanmar, Thailand and Vietnam. Also found in China, India, Sri Lanka and Taiwan.

HABITS AND HABITAT Arboreal and nocturnal species, found up to 1,000m in South-East Asia. Occurs in hilly and lower montane forests, including primary and tall secondary forests, as well as some orchards and plantation forests.

Spotted Giant Flying Squirrel ■ *Petaurista elegans*

HB 34–36.5cm, T 34–36.5cm

DESCRIPTION Variable. Upperparts, including membrane, dark rufous and black with extensive large white spots, underparts pale rufous and tail black (Peninsular Malaysia and Thailand). Elsewhere in the region the upperparts are brown with fewer white spots, mainly on the head and the centre of the back, and the feet and tail are reddish brown. In Java, white spots may be lacking entirely.

DISTRIBUTION Indonesia (Java, Kalimantan, Sumatra), Laos, Malaysia (Peninsular Malaysia, Sabah, Sarawak), Myanmar, Thailand and Vietnam. Also found in Bhutan, China, India and Nepal.

HABITS AND HABITAT Nocturnal and strictly arboreal. Found in hill and montane forests, in tall trees and scrub, as well as on rock cliffs. Nests in tree-hollows.

Red Giant Flying Squirrel ■ *Petaurista petaurista*

HB 40–52cm, T 40–60cm

DESCRIPTION Colour and pattern vary across the range of this species. In Peninsular Malaysia the entire body is dark reddish with a clean-cut black tail tip, feet, nose, chin, eye-ring and behind the ears. In southern Myanmar and western Thailand the colour is similar but there is light speckling on the head and back. Variations in other parts of the range include pale orange upperparts with some speckling, whitish underparts, and a reddish, brownish or grey tail.

DISTRIBUTION Brunei, Indonesia (Java, Kalimantan, Sumatra), Malaysia (Peninsular Malaysia, Sabah, Sarawak), Myanmar and Thailand. Also found in China, India and Nepal. Not seen in Singapore since 1995 and may be extirpated.

HABITS AND HABITAT Arboreal and nocturnal, although occasionally active during the day, especially just before dusk. Occurs in a wide variety of forests from lowlands to mountain tops, including in tall secondary forests. Nests in holes in large trees.

Palawan Flying Squirrel ▪ *Hylopetes nigripes* HB 26–28cm, T 33–36cm

DESCRIPTION Brown in colour, sometimes having prominent white spots. It has a long, bushy dark brown to black tail, and, like all flying squirrels, a membrane used for gliding that extends between the fore and hind limbs. Large eyes assist with vision at night.

DISTRIBUTION Philippines. Found only in the Palawan Faunal Region, on Palawan and the Bancalan islands.

HABITS AND HABITAT Completely nocturnal and arboreal. Found in primary and secondary lowland forest, from sea level to at least 200m. It requires cavities in large trees, where it builds its nests.

NOTES Deforestation may be a serious threat due to this species' reliance on tree cavities – research into this issue is required. It is occasionally hunted for food and captured for the pet trade.

Long-tailed Giant Rat ■ *Leopoldamys sabanus* HB 20–27.5cm, T 27–41.5cm

DESCRIPTION Upperparts buffy brown to orange-brown with darker fur in the dorsal area. Underparts creamy white. Very long tail, dark all around the base and on top, pale tip and underside.

DISTRIBUTION Brunei, Cambodia, Indonesia (Java, Kalimantan, Sumatra), Laos, Malaysia (Peninsular Malaysia, Sabah, Sarawak), Myanmar, Thailand and Vietnam. Also found in Bangladesh and India.

HABITS AND HABITAT Nocturnal and semi-arboreal, foraging on the ground as well as in trees. Found in lowland forest habitats, although up to 3,100m on Mount Kinabalu in Sabah, Malaysia. Feeds on invertebrates, fruit and other vegetable matter.

NOTES The Long-tailed Giant Rat may in fact represent not a single species, but a complex of several similar species.

Palawan Maxomys ▪ *Maxomys panglima* TL 37–41cm, T 18–23cm

DESCRIPTION Upperparts greyish brown to brown. Underparts white. Pink nose and large ears. The scaly tail is dark above and white below. Very spiny fur – more so than any other rat in the Palawan Faunal Region.

DISTRIBUTION Philippines. Endemic to the Palawan Faunal Region on the islands of Balabac, Palawan, Busuanga, Calauit and Culion.

HABITS AND HABITAT Largely nocturnal. Found in primary and secondary forests, as well as in agricultural areas and plantations. Lowlands and low montane habitats to at least 1,550m.

NOTES This is one of the commonest rats in the Palawan Faunal Region.

Red Spiny Maxomys ■ *Maxomys surifer* HB 16–21cm, T 15–21cm

DESCRIPTION Upperparts are a rich orange-brown to reddish brown, contrasting with a white underside, with extensive stiff spines amongst the dorsal and ventral fur. The orange-brown colouring extends under the neck, forming a collar. The very long tail is bicoloured, dark above and light below, and is largely naked. The snout is long and pointed.

DISTRIBUTION Brunei, Cambodia, Indonesia (Java, Kalimantan, Sumatra), Laos, Malaysia (Peninsular Malaysia, Sabah, Sarawak), Myanmar, Thailand and Vietnam. Believed to be extinct in Singapore. Also found in China.

HABITS AND HABITAT Nocturnal and exclusively terrestrial. This species occurs in primary and mature secondary forest, and at forest edges in adjacent cultivated areas. Does not occur in heavily degraded habitats or in large-scale oil-palm plantations.

NOTES There is considerable geographic variation, and more than one species may be represented – more studies are required.

Malaysian Wood Rat ▪ *Rattus tiomanicus* HB 14–19cm, T 15–20cm

DESCRIPTION Upperparts finely grizzled olive-brown with short stiff spines and dark guard hairs. Underparts white. Tail dark brown. Large ears. Foot pads are well adapted for climbing.

DISTRIBUTION Brunei, Indonesia (Java, Kalimantan, Sumatra), Malaysia (Peninsular Malaysia, Sabah, Sarawak), Philippines (the Palawan Faunal Region) and Thailand.

HABITS AND HABITAT Found in a variety of lowland habitats, including secondary forest, agricultural areas, plantations, grassland–forest mosaic, selectively logged forests and rice fields.

NOTES This species climbs well and spends considerable time in trees.

Tanezumi Rat ■ *Rattus tanezumi* HB 10.5–21.5cm, T 12–23cm

DESCRIPTION Upperparts olive-brown to reddish brown, underparts much lighter. The tail is dark grey and mostly naked. The ears are large and the eyes are black. Very similar to the House Rat (*Rattus rattus*) and often lumped together as the same species. However, both these species likely represent a larger species complex.

DISTRIBUTION Cambodia, Laos, Malaysia (Peninsular Malaysia, Sabah, Sarawak), Singapore, Thailand and Vietnam. Introduced in Indonesia and Philippines. Also found in Afghanistan, Bangladesh, Bhutan, China, India, Japan, North and South Korea, Nepal and Taiwan.

HABITS AND HABITAT Nocturnal and sometimes diurnal. Extremely adaptable and commensal with humans, found in many man-made habitats including towns, cities and agricultural areas, feeding on a variety of waste and food scraps, as well as seeds, fruits, insects and some small animals. It is also found in disturbed forests in some areas.

NOTES In some areas, such as the Philippines, this is an extremely destructive introduced pest.

Panay Bushy-tailed Cloud Rat ■ *Crateromys heaneyi*

HB 28–35cm, T 30–40cm

DESCRIPTION Dark brown to reddish brown, with thick, soft fur. The fur on the underparts is shorter and paler, and the fur on the tail is black. The head is broad with a short snout and a 'mask' of greyish fur on the cheeks, and the eyes and ears are proportionately small.

DISTRIBUTION Philippines. Endemic to the Greater Negros–Panay Faunal Region on Panay Island.

HABITS AND HABITAT Nocturnal and arboreal. Dependent on primary and secondary forests. Found up to 400m, but may occur at higher altitudes. Feeds on fruits and leaves. Nests in holes in large trees.

NOTES Severely impacted by habitat destruction due to illegal logging and agricultural encroachment. There is some hunting pressure. Also known as the Panay Cloud Runner, because of its arboreal habits.

East Asian Porcupine ■ *Hystrix brachyura* HB 59–72cm, T 6–11cm

DESCRIPTION Porcupines, well known for their quills, are globally widespread. The East Asian Porcupine has dark brown to black short hair with long quills on the lower back and shorter quills on the back of the neck and the upper back. Thick, hollow quills on the short tail, which rattle when shaken. Quills are black with pale bases and tips. There is a white band on the upper chest and a blunt face.

DISTRIBUTION Brunei, Cambodia, Indonesia (Kalimantan, Sumatra), Laos, Malaysia (Peninsular Malaysia, Sabah, Sarawak), Myanmar, Singapore, Thailand and Vietnam. Also found in Bangladesh, China, India and Nepal.

HABITS AND HABITAT Terrestrial and largely nocturnal. Found in primary and secondary forests, open areas and cultivated land, but always near rocky, hilly areas, where they dig burrows.

NOTES Burrows are frequently found in rugged outcrops and limestone areas, and are most often occupied by family groups.

Palawan Porcupine ■ *Hystrix pumila* HB 49–60cm, T 4–10cm

DESCRIPTION The body and tail are densely covered with quills. The upperparts are dark brown to black, with whitish underparts. It has a short tail, small ears and eyes.

DISTRIBUTION Philippines. Endemic to the Palawan Faunal Region on the islands of Busuanga and Palawan.

HABITS AND HABITAT It is found in mainly lowland primary and secondary forest. It is nocturnal, and while not much is known of its diet, it is thought to feed on similar items to other members of its genus, such as roots and tubers as well as some animal matter. During the day it shelters in underground burrows, typically shared by members of a small family group.

NOTES When threatened, the Palawan Porcupine may raise its quills, making it appear much larger than it really is. If the threat persists, it may stamp its feet, rattle its tail, and eventually charge backwards, using its quills as a weapon.

Long-tailed Porcupine ■ *Trichys fasciculata* HB 37.5–43.5cm, T 15–24cm

DESCRIPTION Upperparts brown, with short, flattened quills. Underparts pale. Quills are dark but whitish towards the base, and cannot be erected. The tail is long and scaly, with a brush of hollow bristles at the end.

DISTRIBUTION Brunei, Indonesia (Kalimantan, Sumatra) and Malaysia (Peninsular Malaysia, Sabah, Sarawak).

HABITS AND HABITAT Found in lowland and lower montane primary forest, as well as secondary and cultivated areas. Spends time foraging on the ground as well as in trees.

NOTES This is the smallest of the region's porcupines and is somewhat rat-like in appearance.

For each species, an '×' indicates presence in a particular country. An asterisk (*) means that the species is possibly extinct in the wild, but this is pending confirmation; historical range countries are provided. Country abbreviations are as follows:

BN   Brunei
KH   Cambodia
ID   Indonesia
LA   Laos
MM Myanmar
MY   Malaysia
PH   Philippines
SG   Singapore
TH   Thailand
VN   Vietnam

The final column shows the IUCN Red List category of each species. The IUCN Red List of Threatened Species is the most comprehensive scientific system for evaluating the conservation status of both plant and animal species, mobilising a global network of scientists and partner organisations. The goal of the Red List is to provide information towards generating action for the conservation of biodiversity. Using rigorous criteria, the IUCN attempts to classify species according to risk level, as follows:

Extinct (EX)
Extinct in the Wild (EW)
Critically Endangered (CR)
Endangered (EN)
Vulnerable (VU)
Near Threatened (NT)
Least Concern (LC)
Data Deficient (DD)
Not Evaluated[†] (NE)

In the checklist, marine mammals are listed separately, because the occurrence of marine mammals in the region is poorly understood, and a country-by-country listing was not feasible given their movements and occurrence in international waters. We have listed the marine mammal species that are generally known from South-East Asian waters.

[†] NE includes species not yet assessed, or possibly not recognised in the Red List.

English name	Scientific name	BN	KH	ID	LA	MM	MY	PH	SG	TH	VN	IUCN
ARTIODACTYLA													
Bovidae													
Gaur	Bos gaurus		x		x	x	x			x	x	VU
Banteng	Bos javanicus		x	x	x	x	x			x	x	EN
Kouprey	Bos sauveli		x*		x*					x*	x*	CR/PE*
Wild Water Buffalo	Bubalus arnee		x			x				x	x	EN
Tamaraw	Bubalus mindorensis							x				CR
Takin	Budorcas taxicolor					x						VU
Indochinese Serow	Capricornis milneedwardsii		x		x	x				x	x	NT
Burmese Red Serow	Capricornis rubidus					x						NT
Sunda Serow	Capricornis sumatraensis			x			x			x		VU
Red Goral	Naemorhedus baileyi					x						VU
Chinese Goral	Naemorhedus griseus					x				x	x	VU
Greater Blue Sheep	Pseudois nayaur					x						LC
Saola	Pseudoryx nghetinhensis				x						x	CR
Cervidae													
Calamian Deer	Axis calamianensis							x				EN
Bawean Deer	Axis kuhlii			x								CR
Hog Deer	Axis porcinus		x			x				x		EN
Sika	Cervus nippon										x	LC
Tufted Deer	Elaphodus cephalophus					x						NT
Bornean Yellow Muntjac	Muntiacus atherodes	x		x			x					LC
Fea's Muntjac	Muntiacus feae					x				x		DD
Gongshan Muntjac	Muntiacus gongshanensis					x						DD
Sumatran Mountain Muntjac	Muntiacus montanus			x								DD
Red Muntjac	Muntiacus muntjak	x	x	x	x	x	x			x	x	LC

English name	Scientific name	BN	KH	ID	LA	MM	MY	PH	SG	TH	VN	IUCN
Puhoat Muntjac	Muntiacus puhoatensis										x	DD
Leaf Muntjac	Muntiacus putaoensis					x						DD
Roosevelts' Muntjac	Muntiacus rooseveltorum				x	x					x	DD
Annamite Muntjac	Muntiacus truongsonensis				x	x					x	DD
Large-antlered Muntjac	Muntiacus vuquangensis				x						x	EN
Eld's Deer	Rucervus eldii					x					x	EN
Philippine Spotted Deer	Rusa alfredi							x				EN
Philippine Brown Deer	Rusa mariana							x				VU
Javan Rusa	Rusa timorensis			x								VU
Sambar	Rusa unicolor	x	x	x	x	x	x			x	x	VU
Moschidae												
Forest Musk-deer	Moschus berezovskii										x	EN
Black Musk-deer	Moschus fuscus					x						EN
Suidae												
Palawan Bearded Pig	Sus ahoenobarbus							x				VU
Sunda Bearded Pig	Sus barbatus	x		x			x					VU
Heude's Pig	Sus bucculentus				x						x	DD
Visayan Warty Pig	Sus cebifrons							x				CR
Oliver's Warty Pig	Sus oliveri							x				EN
Philippine Warty Pig	Sus philippensis							x				VU
Eurasian Wild Pig	Sus scrofa		x	x	x	x	x		x	x	x	LC
Javan Warty Pig	Sus verrucosus			x								EN
Tragulidae												
Javan Chevrotain	Tragulus javanicus			x								DD
Lesser Oriental Chevrotain	Tragulus kanchil	x	x	x	x	x	x		x	x	x	LC
Greater Oriental Chevrotain	Tragulus napu	x		x	x	x	x		x	x		LC
Balabac Chevrotain	Tragulus nigricans							x				EN

English name	Scientific name	BN	KH	ID	LA	MM	MY	PH	SG	TH	VN	IUCN
Silver-backed Chevrotain	Tragulus versicolor										x	DD
Williamson's Chevrotain	Tragulus williamsoni									x		DD
CARNIVORA												
Ailuridae												
Red Panda	Ailurus fulgens					x						VU
Canidae												
Golden Jackal	Canis aureus		x		x	x				x	x	LC
Dhole	Cuon alpinus		x	x	x	x	x			x	x	EN
Raccoon Dog	Nyctereutes procyonoides										x	LC
Red Fox	Vulpes vulpes										x	LC
Felidae												
Bay Cat	Catopuma badia			x		x	x					EN
Asian Golden Cat	Catopuma temminckii		x	x	x	x	x			x	x	NT
Jungle Cat	Felis chaus		x		x	x				x	x	LC
Sunda Clouded Leopard	Neofelis diardi	x		x			x					VU
Clouded Leopard	Neofelis nebulosa		x		x	x	x			x	x	VU
Leopard	Panthera pardus		x	x	x	x	x			x	x	NT
Tiger	Panthera tigris		x	x	x	x	x			x	x	EN
Marbled Cat	Pardofelis marmorata	x	x	x	x	x	x			x	x	VU
Leopard Cat	Prionailurus bengalensis	x	x	x	x	x	x	x	x	x	x	LC
Flat-headed Cat	Prionailurus planiceps	x		x			x			x		EN
Fishing Cat	Prionailurus viverrinus		x	x	x	x	x			x	x	EN
Herpestidae												
Short-tailed Mongoose	Herpestes brachyurus	x		x			x	x				LC
Small Asian Mongoose	Herpestes javanicus		x	x	x	x	x			x	x	LC
Collared Mongoose	Herpestes semitorquatus	x		x			x					DD
Crab-eating Mongoose	Herpestes urva		x		x	x	x			x	x	LC

English name	Scientific name	BN	KH	ID	LA	MM	MY	PH	SG	TH	VN	IUCN
Mustelidae												
Oriental Small-clawed Otter	*Aonyx cinereus*	×	×	×	×	×	×	×	×	×	×	VU
Greater Hog Badger	*Arctonyx collaris*		×		×	×					×	NT
Sumatran Hog Badger	*Arctonyx hoevenii*			×								NE
Eurasian Otter	*Lutra lutra*		×	×	×	×				×	×	NT
Hairy-nosed Otter	*Lutra sumatrana*	×	×	×	×	×	×			×	×	EN
Smooth Otter	*Lutrogale perspicillata*	×	×	×	×	×	×		×	×	×	VU
Yellow-throated Marten	*Martes flavigula*	×	×	×	×	×	×			×	×	LC
Stone Marten	*Martes foina*					×						LC
Bornean Ferret Badger	*Melogale everetti*						×					DD
Small-toothed Ferret Badger	*Melogale moschata*				×	×					×	LC
Javan Ferret Badger	*Melogale orientalis*			×								DD
Large-toothed Ferret Badger	*Melogale personata*		×		×	×				×	×	DD
Cuc Phuong Ferret Badger	*Melogale cucphuongensis*										×	NE
Yellow-bellied Weasel	*Mustela kathiah*				×	×				×	×	LC
Indonesian Mountain Weasel	*Mustela lutreolina*			×								DD
Least Weasel	*Mustela nivalis*										×	LC
Malay Weasel	*Mustela nudipes*	×		×			×			×		LC
Siberian Weasel	*Mustela sibirica*				×	×				×		LC
Stripe-backed Weasel	*Mustela strigidorsa*				×	×				×	×	LC
Mephitidae												
Sunda Stink-badger	*Mydaus javanensis*			×			×					LC
Palawan Stink-badger	*Mydaus marchei*							×				LC
Ursidae												
Sun Bear	*Helarctos malayanus*	×	×	×	×	×	×			×	×	VU
Asian Black Bear	*Ursus thibetanus*		×	×	×	×				×	×	VU

English name	Scientific name	BN	KH	ID	LA	MM	MY	PH	SG	TH	VN	IUCN
Viverridae												
Binturong	*Arctictis binturong*	×	×	×	×	×	×	×		×	×	VU
Small-toothed Palm Civet	*Arctogalidia trivirgata*	×	×	×	×	×	×		×	×	×	LC
Owston's Civet	*Chrotogale owstoni*				×						×	VU
Otter Civet	*Cynogale bennettii*	×		×			×			×		EN
Hose's Civet	*Diplogale hosei*	×		×			×					VU
Banded Civet	*Hemigalus derbyanus*			×			×			×		VU
Masked Palm Civet	*Paguma larvata*	×	×	×	×	×	×	×		×	×	LC
Common Palm Civet	*Paradoxurus hermaphroditus*	×	×	×	×	×	×	×	×	×	×	LC
Large-spotted Civet	*Viverra megaspila*				×	×	×			×	×	VU
Malay Civet	*Viverra tangalunga*	×		×			×	×	×			LC
Large Indian Civet	*Viverra zibetha*		×		×	×	×			×	×	NT
Small Indian Civet	*Viverricula indica*		×	×	×	×	×			×	×	LC
Prionodontidae												
Banded Linsang	*Prionodon linsang*	×		×		×	×			×		LC
Spotted Linsang	*Prionodon pardicolor*		×		×	×				×	×	LC
CHIROPTERA												
Craseonycteridae												
Kitti's Hog-nosed Bat	*Craseonycteris thonglongyai*					×				×		VU
Emballonuridae												
Small Asian Sheath-tailed Bat	*Emballonura alecto*	×		×			×	×				LC
Lesser Sheath-tailed Bat	*Emballonura monticola*	×		×			×		×	×		LC
Pouched Tomb Bat	*Saccolaimus saccolaimus*	×		×		×	×	×	×	×	×	LC
Long-winged Tomb Bat	*Taphozous longimanus*	×		×		×	×			×		LC
Black-bearded Tomb Bat	*Taphozous melanopogon*	×	×	×	×	×	×	×	×	×	×	LC
Naked-rumped Tomb Bat	*Taphozous nudiventris*					×						LC
Theobald's Tomb Bat	*Taphozous theobaldi*		×		×	×				×	×	LC

Hipposideridae

English name	Scientific name	BN	KH	ID	LA	MM	MY	PH	SG	TH	VN	IUCN
Trident Roundleaf Bat	Aselliscus stoliczkanus				×	×	×			×	×	LC
Asian Tailless Roundleaf Bat	Coelops frithii		×	×	×	×	×			×	×	LC
Philippine Tailless Roundleaf Bat	Coelops hirsutus							×				DD
Malaysian Tailless Roundleaf Bat	Coelops robinsoni			×			×			×		VU
Great Roundleaf Bat	Hipposideros armiger				×	×	×	×		×	×	LC
Dusky Roundleaf Bat	Hipposideros ater	×	×	×			×	×		×		LC
Bicoloured Roundleaf Bat	Hipposideros bicolor	×		×			×	×	×			LC
Short-headed Roundleaf Bat	Hipposideros breviceps			×								DD
Fawn Roundleaf Bat	Hipposideros cervinus	×		×	×	×	×	×				LC
Ashy Roundleaf Bat	Hipposideros cineraceus	×	×	×	×	×	×			×	×	LC
Large Mindanao Roundleaf Bat	Hipposideros coronatus							×				DD
Cox's Roundleaf Bat	Hipposideros coxi						×					DD
Diadem Roundleaf Bat	Hipposideros diadema	×	×	×	×	×	×	×		×	×	LC
Least Roundleaf Bat	Hipposideros doriae	×		×			×					NT
Dyak Roundleaf Bat	Hipposideros dyacorum	×		×			×					LC
Cantor's Roundleaf Bat	Hipposideros galeritus	×	×	×	×		×			×	×	LC
Grand Roundleaf Bat	Hipposideros grandis					×				×	×	DD
Griffin's Roundleaf Bat	Hipposideros griffini										×	NE
Thailand Roundleaf Bat	Hipposideros halophyllus									×		EN
Khaokhouay Roundleaf Bat	Hipposideros khaokhouayensis				×							VU
Intermediate Roundleaf Bat	Hipposideros larvatus		×	×	×	×	×			×	×	LC
Boonsong's Roundleaf Bat	Hipposideros lekaguli					×	×	×		×		NT
Shield-faced Roundleaf Bat	Hipposideros lylei					×	×			×	×	LC
Maduran Roundleaf Bat	Hipposideros madurae			×								LC
Malayan Roundleaf Bat	Hipposideros nequam						×					DD
Philippine Forest Roundleaf Bat	Hipposideros obscurus							×				LC
Orbiculus Roundleaf Bat	Hipposideros orbiculus			×			×					EN

English name	Scientific name	BN	KH	ID	LA	MM	MY	PH	SG	TH	VN	IUCN
Large-eared Roundleaf Bat	Hipposideros pomona				x	x	x			x	x	LC
Pratt's Roundleaf Bat	Hipposideros pratti					x	x				x	LC
Philippine Pygmy Roundleaf Bat	Hipposideros pygmaeus							x				LC
Ridley's Roundleaf Bat	Hipposideros ridleyi	x					x		x	x		VU
Annamite Roundleaf Bat	Hipposideros rotalis				x							LC
Shield-nosed Roundleaf Bat	Hipposideros scutinares				x						x	VU
Sorensen's Roundleaf Bat	Hipposideros sorenseni			x								VU
Lesser Roundleaf Bat	Hipposideros turpis									x	x	NT
Large-eared Tailless Roundleaf Bat	Paracoelops megalotis										x	DD
Megadermatidae												
Greater False-vampire	Megaderma lyra		x		x	x	x	x		x	x	LC
Lesser False-vampire	Megaderma spasma	x	x	x	x	x	x	x	x	x	x	LC
Molossidae												
Lesser Naked Bat	Cheiromeles parvidens							x				LC
Greater Naked Bat	Cheiromeles torquatus	x		x			x	x	x	x		LC
Sumatran Mastiff Bat	Mormopterus doriae			x								DD
Java Giant Mastiff Bat	Otomops formosus			x								DD
Wroughton's Giant Mastiff Bat	Otomops wroughtoni		x									DD
Johor Wrinkle-lipped Bat	Tadarida johorensis			x			x					VU
La Touche's Free-tailed Bat	Tadarida latouchei				x							DD
Sunda Free-tailed Bat	Tadarida mops	x		x			x			x		NT
Asian Wrinkle-lipped Bat	Tadarida plicata	x	x	x	x	x	x	x		x	x	LC
Sulawesi Free-tailed Bat	Tadarida sarasinorum			x				x				DD
Nycteridae												
Javan Slit-faced Bat	Nycteris javanica			x								VU
Malayan Slit-faced Bat	Nycteris tragata	x		x			x		x	x		NT

English name	Scientific name	BN	KH	ID	LA	MM	MY	PH	SG	TH	VN	IUCN
Pteropodidae												
Golden-crowned Flying-fox	*Acerodon jubatus*							×				EN
Palawan Flying-fox	*Acerodon leucotis*							×				VU
Bornean Fruit Bat	*Aethalops aequalis*	×					×					LC
Grey Fruit Bat	*Aethalops alecto*			×			×					LC
Mindanao Fruit Bat	*Alionycteris paucidentata*							×				LC
Spotted-winged Fruit Bat	*Balionycteris maculata*	×		×			×			×		LC
Black-capped Fruit Bat	*Chironax melanocephalus*	×		×			×			×		LC
Short-nosed Fruit Bat	*Cynopterus brachyotis*	×		×	×	×	×	×	×	×	×	LC
Horsfield's Fruit Bat	*Cynopterus horsfieldii*	×	×	×	×					×	×	LC
Peters's Fruit Bat	*Cynopterus luzoniensis*								×			LC
Minute Fruit Bat	*Cynopterus minutus*	×		×								LC
Greater Short-nosed Fruit Bat	*Cynopterus sphinx*		×	×	×	×	×		×	×	×	LC
Indonesian Short-nosed Fruit Bat	*Cynopterus titthaecheilus*			×								CR
Negros Naked-backed Fruit Bat	*Dobsonia chapmani*							×				VU
Brooks's Dayak Fruit Bat	*Dyacopterus brooksi*			×								NT
Dayak Fruit Bat	*Dyacopterus spadiceus*	×		×			×	×		×		NT
Philippine Large-headed Fruit Bat	*Dyacopterus rickarti*								×			NE
Greater Nectar Bat	*Eonycteris major*	×		×								DD
Philippine Nectar Bat	*Eonycteris robusta*							×				NT
Cave Nectar Bat	*Eonycteris spelaea*	×		×	×			×	×	×	×	LC
Philippine Pygmy Fruit Bat	*Haplonycteris fischeri*							×				LC
Harpy Fruit Bat	*Harpyionycteris whiteheadi*							×				VU
Lesser Long-tongued Nectar Bat	*Macroglossus minimus*	×	×	×			×	×	×	×	×	LC
Greater Long-tongued Nectar Bat	*Macroglossus sobrinus*		×	×	×	×	×			×	×	LC
Sunda Tailless Fruit Bat	*Megaerops ecaudatus*	×		×			×			×		LC
Javan Tailless Fruit Bat	*Megaerops kusnotoi*			×								VU
Northern Tailless Fruit Bat	*Megaerops niphanae*				×					×	×	LC

English name	Scientific name	BN	KH	ID	LA	MM	MY	PH	SG	TH	VN	IUCN
White-collared Fruit Bat	*Megaerops wetmorei*	×		×			×	×				VU
Philippine Tube-nosed Fruit Bat	*Nyctimene rabori*							×				EN
Luzon Fruit Bat	*Otopteropus cartilagonodus*							×	×			LC
Dusky Fruit Bat	*Penthetor lucasi*	×		×			×	×	×	×		LC
Greater Musky Fruit Bat	*Ptenochirus jagori*							×				LC
Lesser Musky Fruit Bat	*Ptenochirus minor*							×				LC
Ryukyu Flying-fox	*Pteropus dasymallus*							×				NT
Indian Flying-fox	*Pteropus giganteus*					×						LC
Island Flying-fox	*Pteropus hypomelanus*		×	×		×		×		×	×	LC
White-winged Flying-fox	*Pteropus leucopterus*							×				LC
Lyle's Flying-fox	*Pteropus lylei*		×							×	×	VU
Black-eared Flying-fox	*Pteropus melanotus*		×	×								VU
Little Golden-mantled Flying-fox	*Pteropus pumilus*											NT
Philippine Grey Flying-fox	*Pteropus speciosus*			×				×				DD
Large Flying-fox	*Pteropus vampyrus*	×	×	×	×		×	×	×	×	×	NT
Geoffroy's Rousette	*Rousettus amplexicaudatus*	×	×	×	×	×	×	×	×	×	×	LC
Leschenault's Rousette	*Rousettus leschenaultii*		×	×	×	×	×			×	×	LC
Bare-backed Rousette	*Rousettus spinalatus*	×		×			×					VU
Hill Fruit Bat	*Sphaerias blanfordi*					×				×	×	NE
Wallace's Stripe-faced Fruit Bat	*Styloctenium mindorensis*							×				DD
Rhinolophidae												
Acuminate Horseshoe Bat	*Rhinolophus acuminatus*	×	×	×	×	×	×	×		×	×	LC
Intermediate Horseshoe Bat	*Rhinolophus affinis*		×	×	×	×	×			×	×	LC
Arcuate Horseshoe Bat	*Rhinolophus arcuatus*			×			×	×				LC
Bornean Horseshoe Bat	*Rhinolophus borneensis*	×	×	×	×		×				×	LC
Canute's Horseshoe Bat	*Rhinolophus canuti*			×								VU
Sulawesi Horseshoe Bat	*Rhinolophus celebensis*			×								LC
Indochinese Horseshoe Bat	*Rhinolophus chaseni*		×		×						×	NE

English name	Scientific name	BN	KH	ID	LA	MM	MY	PH	SG	TH	VN	IUCN
Croslet Horseshoe Bat	*Rhinolophus coelophyllus*				×	×	×			×		LC
Convex Horseshoe Bat	*Rhinolophus convexus*				×	×	×					DD
Creagh's Horseshoe Bat	*Rhinolophus creaghi*	×		×								LC
Philippine Forest Horseshoe Bat	*Rhinolophus inops*							×				LC
Blyth's Horseshoe Bat	*Rhinolophus lepidus*		×	×	×	×	×		×	×	×	LC
Great Woolly Horseshoe Bat	*Rhinolophus luctus*		×	×	×	×	×		×	×	×	LC
Big-eared Horseshoe Bat	*Rhinolophus macrotis*			×	×	×	×	×		×	×	LC
Madura Horseshoe Bat	*Rhinolophus madurensis*			×								EN
Malayan Horseshoe Bat	*Rhinolophus malayanus*		×		×	×	×			×	×	LC
Marshall's Horseshoe Bat	*Rhinolophus marshalli*				×	×	×			×	×	LC
	Rhinolophus microglobosus		×									NE
Bourret's Horseshoe Bat	*Rhinolophus paradoxolophus*				×					×	×	LC
Pearson's Horseshoe Bat	*Rhinolophus pearsonii*				×	×				×	×	LC
Enormous-eared Horseshoe Bat	*Rhinolophus philippinensis*	×		×			×	×			×	LC
Least Horseshoe Bat	*Rhinolophus pusillus*		×	×	×	×	×			×		LC
Peninsular Horseshoe Bat	*Rhinolophus robinsoni*						×			×		NT
Rufous Horseshoe Bat	*Rhinolophus rouxii*					×						LC
Large Rufous Horseshoe Bat	*Rhinolophus rufus*	×						×				NT
Lesser Woolly Horseshoe Bat	*Rhinolophus sedulus*	×	×	×			×					NT
Shamel's Horseshoe Bat	*Rhinolophus shameli*		×		×	×	×			×	×	LC
Shorrtridge's Horseshoe Bat	*Rhinolophus shortridgei*					×						LC
Thai Horseshoe Bat	*Rhinolophus siamensis*				×							LC
Chinese Horseshoe Bat	*Rhinolophus sinicus*					×				×	×	DD
Lesser Brown Horseshoe Bat	*Rhinolophus stheno*		×	×	×	×	×			×	×	LC
Little Nepalese Horseshoe Bat	*Rhinolophus subbadius*					×						LC
Small Rufous Horseshoe Bat	*Rhinolophus subrufus*							×				DD
Thomas's Horseshoe Bat	*Rhinolophus thomasi*				×	×				×	×	LC
Trefoil Horseshoe Bat	*Rhinolophus trifoliatus*	×		×		×	×		×	×		LC

English name	Scientific name	BN	KH	ID	LA	MM	MY	PH	SG	TH	VN	IUCN
Yellow-faced Horseshoe Bat	Rhinolophus virgo											LC
Dobson's Horseshoe Bat	Rhinolophus yunanensis		×			×				×		LC
Rhinopomatidae												
Lesser Mouse-tailed Bat	Rhinopoma hardwickii									×	×	LC
Greater Mouse-tailed Bat	Rhinopoma microphyllum			×						×	×	LC
Vespertilionidae												
Collared Pipistrelle	Arielulus aureocollaris				×					×	×	LC
Black Gilded Pipistrelle	Arielulus circumdatus		×									LC
Coppery Pipistrelle	Arielulus cuprosus						×					DD
Social Pipistrelle	Arielulus societatis						×					VU
Eastern Barbastelle	Barbastella darjelingensis				×							NE
Surat Serotine	Eptesicus dimissus									×		DD
Thick-eared Serotine	Eptesicus pachyotis					×				×		LC
Eurasian Serotine	Eptesicus serotinus				×	×				×	×	LC
Disc-footed Bat	Eudiscopus denticulus				×	×				×	×	DD
Chocolate Pipistrelle	Falsistrellus affinis					×						LC
Pungent Pipistrelle	Falsistrellus mordax			×								DD
Peters's Pipistrelle	Falsistrellus petersi			×			×	×				DD
Javan Thick-thumbed Pipistrelle	Glischropus javanus			×								DD
Common Thick-thumbed Pipistrelle	Glischropus tylopus	×	×	×	×	×	×	×		×	×	LC
Lesser Hairy-winged Bat	Harpiocephalus harpia		×	×	×	×	×	×		×	×	LC
Greater Hairy-winged Bat	Harpiocephalus mordax				×	×	×			×	×	DD
Least False-serotine	Hesperoptenus blanfordi		×	×	×	×	×			×	×	LC
Doria's False-serotine	Hesperoptenus doriae						×					DD
Tickell's False-serotine	Hesperoptenus tickelli		×		×	×				×	×	LC
Tomes's False-serotine	Hesperoptenus tomesi						×			×		VU
Great Evening Bat	Ia io				×	×				×	×	LC

English name	Scientific name	BN	KH	ID	LA	MM	MY	PH	SG	TH	VN	IUCN
Flores Woolly Bat	*Kerivoula flora*			×			×					VU
Hardwicke's Woolly Bat	*Kerivoula hardwickii*	×	×	×	×	×	×	×	×	×	×	LC
Small Woolly Bat	*Kerivoula intermedia*	×		×			×					NT
Kachin Woolly Bat	*Kerivoula kachinensis*		×		×	×				×	×	LC
Krau Woolly Bat	*Kerivoula krauensis*						×					DD
Indian Woolly Bat	*Kerivoula lenis*	×		×			×					LC
Least Woolly Bat	*Kerivoula minuta*	×		×			×			×		NT
Papillose Woolly Bat	*Kerivoula papillosa*	×	×	×	×		×	×		×	×	LC
Clear-winged Woolly Bat	*Kerivoula pellucida*	×		×			×	×		×		NT
Painted Woolly Bat	*Kerivoula picta*		×	×	×	×	×			×	×	LC
Titania's Woolly Bat	*Kerivoula titania*		×	×	×	×	×			×	×	LC
Whitehead's Woolly Bat	*Kerivoula whiteheadi*	×		×			×	×		×		LC
Little Bent-winged Bat	*Miniopterus australis*	×		×			×	×				LC
Large Bent-winged Bat	*Miniopterus magnater*		×		×	×	×			×	×	LC
Medium Bent-winged Bat	*Miniopterus medius*			×			×			×		LC
Philippine Bent-winged Bat	*Miniopterus paululus*			×				×				DD
Small Bent-winged Bat	*Miniopterus pusillus*		×	×	×	×	×		×	×	×	LC
Common Bent-winged Bat	*Miniopterus schreibersii*		×		×	×	×	×		×	×	NT
Great Bent-winged Bat	*Miniopterus tristis*							×				LC
Bronzed Tube-nosed Bat	*Murina aenea*	×					×			×		VU
Golden Tube-nosed Bat	*Murina aurata*				×	×				×	×	LC
Round-eared Tube-nosed Bat	*Murina cyclotis*	×	×	×	×	×	×	×		×	×	LC
Harrison's Tube-nosed Bat	*Murina harrisoni*		×									DD
Hutton's Tube-nosed Bat	*Murina huttoni*				×	×				×	×	LC
Greater Tube-nosed Bat	*Murina leucogaster*											DD
Rozendaal's Tube-nosed Bat	*Murina rozendaali*	×					×					VU
Lesser Tube-nosed Bat	*Murina suilla*	×		×			×		×	×		LC

152

English name	Scientific name	BN	KH	ID	LA	MM	MY	PH	SG	TH	VN	IUCN
Scully's Tube-nosed Bat	Murina tubinaris				×	×				×	×	LC
Grey Large-footed Myotis	Myotis adversus			×			×		×			LC
Szechuan Myotis	Myotis altarium									×		LC
Annamite Myotis	Myotis annamiticus				×						×	DD
Hairy-faced Myotis	Myotis annectans		×		×					×	×	LC
Peters's Myotis	Myotis ater	×		×			×	×		×	×	LC
Chinese Myotis	Myotis chinensis					×					×	LC
Black-and-orange Myotis	Myotis formosus			×			×	×			×	LC
Gomantong Myotis	Myotis gomantongensis			×			×					LC
Van Hasselt's Myotis	Myotis hasseltii	×	×	×		×	×			×	×	LC
Herman's Myotis	Myotis hermani			×			×			×		DD
Horsfield's Myotis	Myotis horsfieldii		×	×	×	×	×	×		×	×	LC
Indochinese Myotis	Myotis laniger				×						×	LC
Philippine Large-footed Myotis	Myotis macrotarsus			×			×	×				NT
Large Brown Myotis	Myotis montivagus		×	×	×	×	×			×	×	LC
Asian Whiskered Myotis	Myotis muricola	×	×	×	×	×	×	×	×	×	×	LC
Eurasian Whiskered Myotis	Myotis mystacinus					×						LC
Singapore Myotis	Myotis oreias								×			DD
Rickett's Myotis	Myotis pilosus				×							NT
Ridley's Myotis	Myotis ridleyi	×		×			×			×	×	NT
Thick-thumbed Myotis	Myotis rosseti		×		×					×	×	LC
Orange-fingered Myotis	Myotis rufopictus							×				DD
Small-toothed Myotis	Myotis siligorensis		×	×	×	×	×			×	×	LC
Eurasian Noctule	Nyctalus noctula					×						LC
Narrow-winged Brown Bat	Philetor brachypterus	×		×			×	×			×	LC
Lesser Groove-toothed Bat	Phoniscus atrox	×		×			×			×		NT
Greater Groove-toothed Bat	Phoniscus jagorii	×		×	×		×	×		×	×	LC

English name	Scientific name	BN	KH	ID	LA	MM	MY	PH	SG	TH	VN	IUCN
Japanese Pipistrelle	Pipistrellus abramus					×					×	LC
Anthony's Pipistrelle	Pipistrellus anthonyi					×						DD
Cadorna's Pipistrelle	Pipistrellus cadornae				×	×					×	LC
Kelaart's Pipistrelle	Pipistrellus ceylonicus			×	×	×	×			×	×	LC
Coromandel Pipistrele	Pipistrellus coromandra		×	×	×	×	×			×	×	LC
Imbricate Pipistrelle	Pipistrellus imbricatus			×			×					LC
Javan Pipistrelle	Pipistrellus javanicus	×	×	×	×	×	×	×	×	×	×	LC
Joffre's Pipistrelle	Pipistrellus joffrei					×						DD
Red-brown Pipistrelle	Pipistrellus kitcheneri			×								DD
Myanmar Pipistrelle	Pipistrellus lophurus					×						DD
Big-eared Pipistrelle	Pipistrellus macrotis			×			×					DD
Mount Popa Pipistrelle	Pipistrellus paterculus				×	×					×	LC
Chinese Pipistrelle	Pipistrellus pulveratus				×	×				×	×	LC
Narrow-winged Pipistrelle	Pipistrellus stenopterus			×			×	×	×	×		LC
Least Pipistrelle	Pipistrellus tenuis	×	×	×	×	×	×	×		×	×	LC
White-winged Pipistrelle	Pipistrellus vordermanni	×		×								DD
Harlequin Bat	Scotomanes ornatus				×	×				×	×	LC
Sody's Yellow House Bat	Scotophilus collinus		×				×					LC
Greater Asian House Bat	Scotophilus heathii		×		×	×	×		×	×	×	LC
Lesser Asian House Bat	Scotophilus kuhlii	×	×	×	×	×	×	×	×	×	×	LC
Lesser Bamboo Bat	Tylonycteris pachypus	×	×	×	×	×	×	×	×	×	×	LC
Greater Bamboo Bat	Tylonycteris robustula	×	×	×	×	×	×	×	×	×	×	LC

DERMOPTERA

Cynocephalidae

English name	Scientific name	BN	KH	ID	LA	MM	MY	PH	SG	TH	VN	IUCN
Philippine Colugo	Cynocephalus volans							×				LC
Sunda Colugo	Galeopterus variegatus	×	×	×	×	×	×		×	×	×	LC

English name	Scientific name	BN	KH	ID	LA	MM	MY	PH	SG	TH	VN	IUCN
INSECTIVORA												
Erinaceidae												
Moonrat	*Echinosorex gymnura*	×		×		×	×			×	×	LC
Large-eared Gymnure	*Hylomys megalotis*				×							DD
Dwarf Gymnure	*Hylomys parvus*			×								VU
Short-tailed Gymnure	*Hylomys suillus*	×	×	×	×	×	×			×	×	LC
Chinese Gymnure	*Neotetracus sinensis*					×					×	LC
Dinagat Gymnure	*Podogymnura aureospinula*							×				EN
Mindanao Gymnure	*Podogymnura truei*							×				LC
Soricidae												
Mole Shrew	*Anourosorex squamipes*				×	×				×	×	LC
Indochinese Short-tailed Shrew	*Blarinella griselda*										×	LC
Myanmar Short-tailed Shrew	*Blarinella wardi*					×						LC
Malayan Water Shrew	*Chimarrogale hantu*						×					NT
Himalayan Water Shrew	*Chimarrogale himalayica*				×	×					×	LC
Sunda Water Shrew	*Chimarrogale phaeura*						×					EN
Styan's Water Shrew	*Chimarrogale styani*					×						LC
Sumatran Water Shrew	*Chimarrogale sumatrana*			×								DD
Cao Van Sung's Shrew	*Chodsigoa caovansunga*										×	DD
Lowe's Shrew	*Chodsigoa parca*					×				×	×	LC
Grey Shrew	*Crocidura attenuata*		×		×	×	×	×		×	×	LC
Kinabalu Shrew	*Crocidura baluensis*						×					VU
Batak Shrew	*Crocidura batakorum*							×				NE
Lesser Mindanao Shrew	*Crocidura beatus*							×				LC
Beccari's Shrew	*Crocidura beccarii*			×								LC
Thick-tailed Shrew	*Crocidura brunnea*			×								LC
Bornean Shrew	*Crocidura foetida*			×			×					LC

English name	Scientific name	BN	KH	ID	LA	MM	MY	PH	SG	TH	VN	IUCN
South-east Asian Shrew	Crocidura fuliginosa		×		×	×	×		×	×	×	LC
Greater Mindanao Shrew	Crocidura grandis							×				DD
Luzon Shrew	Crocidura grayi							×				LC
Hill's Shrew	Crocidura hilliana				×					×		DD
Hutan Shrew	Crocidura hutanis			×								LC
Indochinese Shrew	Crocidura indochinensis				×	×				×	×	LC
Ke Go Shrew	Crocidura kegoensis										×	NE
Sumatran Giant Shrew	Crocidura lepidura											LC
Malayan Shrew	Crocidura malayana						×			×		LC
Javanese Shrew	Crocidura maxi			×								LC
Mindoro Shrew	Crocidura mindorus							×				DD
Sunda Shrew	Crocidura monticola	×		×			×			×		LC
Peninsular Shrew	Crocidura negligens					×				×		LC
Negros Shrew	Crocidura negrina							×				EN
Palawan Shrew	Crocidura palawanensis							×				LC
Panay Shrew	Crocidura panayensis							×				NE
Sumatran Long-tailed Shrew	Crocidura paradoxura			×								LC
Chinese Shrew	Crocidura rapax					×						DD
Voracious Shrew	Crocidura vorax				×						×	LC
Banka Shrew	Crocidura vosmaeri			×								DD
Wuchih Shrew	Crocidura wuchihensis										×	DD
Bailey's Brown-toothed Shrew	Episoriculus baileyi					×					×	NE
Hodgson's Brown-toothed Shrew	Episoriculus caudatus					×						LC
Long-tailed Brown-toothed Shrew	Episoriculus macrurus					×					×	LC
Web-footed Water Shrew	Nectogale elegans					×						LC
Lesser Stripe-backed Shrew	Sorex bedfordiae					×						LC
Black Shrew	Suncus ater						×					DD
Pygmy White-toothed Shrew	Suncus etruscus				×		×			×	×	LC

English name	Scientific name	BN	KH	ID	LA	MM	MY	PH	SG	TH	VN	IUCN
Hose's Shrew	Suncus hosei						x					DD
House Shrew	Suncus murinus	x	x	x	x	x	x		x	x	x	LC
Talpidae												
Large Chinese Mole	Euroscaptor grandis				x	x					x	LC
Kloss's Mole	Euroscaptor klossi				x	x	x			x	x	LC
Long-nosed Chinese Mole	Euroscaptor longirostris										x	LC
Small-toothed Mole	Euroscaptor parvidens										x	DD
Blyth's Mole	Parascaptor leucura					x						LC
Long-tailed Mole	Scaptonyx fusicauda					x					x	LC
Slender Shrew Mole	Uropsilus gracilis					x						LC
LAGOMORPHA												
Leporidae												
Burmese Hare	Lepus peguensis		x		x	x				x	x	LC
Chinese Hare	Lepus sinensis										x	LC
Sumatran Striped Rabbit	Nesolagus netscheri			x								VU
Annamite Striped Rabbit	Nesolagus timminsi				x						x	DD
Ochotonidae												
Forrest's Pika	Ochotona forresti					x						LC
Mountain Pika	Ochotona thibetana					x						LC
PERISSODACTYLA												
Rhinocerotidae												
Sumatran Rhinoceros	Dicerorhinus sumatrensis			x		x	x					CR
Javan Rhinoceros	Rhinoceros sondaicus			x								CR
Tapiridae												
Asian Tapir	Tapirus indicus			x		x	x			x		EN

PHOLIDOTA

Manidae

English name	Scientific name	BN	KH	ID	LA	MM	MY	PH	SG	TH	VN	IUCN
Philippine Pangolin	Manis culionensis							x				NT
Sunda Pangolin	Manis javanica	x	x	x	x	x	x		x	x	x	EN
Chinese Pangolin	Manis pentadactyla				x	x				x	x	EN

PRIMATES

Cercopithecidae

English name	Scientific name	BN	KH	ID	LA	MM	MY	PH	SG	TH	VN	IUCN
Stump-tailed Macaque	Macaca arctoides				x	x	x			x	x	VU
Assamese Macaque	Macaca assamensis				x	x				x	x	NT
Long-tailed Macaque	Macaca fascicularis	x	x	x	x	x	x	x	x	x	x	LC
Northern Pig-tailed Macaque	Macaca leonina		x		x	x	x			x	x	VU
Rhesus Macaque	Macaca mulatta				x	x				x	x	LC
Southern Pig-tailed Macaque	Macaca nemestrina	x		x			x			x		VU
Pagai Island Macaque	Macaca pagensis			x								CR
Siberut Macaque	Macaca siberu			x								VU
Proboscis Monkey	Nasalis larvatus	x		x								EN
Bornean Banded Langur	Presbytis chrysomelas	x		x			x					CR
Javan Grizzled Langur	Presbytis comata			x								EN
Common Banded Langur	Presbytis femoralis			x			x		x	x		NT
White-fronted Langur	Presbytis frontata			x			x					VU
Hose's Langur	Presbytis hosei	x		x			x					VU
Mitred Langur	Presbytis melalophos			x								EN
Natuna Langur	Presbytis natunae			x								VU
Mentawai Langur	Presbytis potenziani			x								EN
Maroon Langur	Presbytis rubicunda			x			x					LC
White-thighed Langur	Presbytis siamensis			x			x			x		NT
Thomas's Langur	Presbytis thomasi			x								VU

English name	Scientific name	BN	KH	ID	LA	MM	MY	PH	SG	TH	VN	IUCN
Grey-shanked Douc	Pygathrix cinerea										x	CR
Red-shanked Douc	Pygathrix nemaeus		x		x						x	EN
Black-shanked Douc	Pygathrix nigripes		x								x	EN
Tonkin Snub-nosed Monkey	Rhinopithecus avunculus										x	CR
Myanmar Snub-nosed Monkey	Rhinopithecus strykeri					x						CR
Simakobu	Simias concolor			x								CR
Javan Langur	Trachypithecus auratus			x								VU
Temasserim Langur	Trachypithecus barbei					x				x		DD
Sundaic Silvered Langur	Trachypithecus cristatus	x		x			x					NT
Delacour's Langur	Trachypithecus delacouri										x	CR
François's Langur	Trachypithecus francoisi										x	EN
Indochinese Silvered Langur	Trachypithecus germaini		x		x	x				x	x	EN
Hatinh Langur	Trachypithecus hatinhensis				x						x	EN
Lao Langur	Trachypithecus laotum				x							VU
Dusky Langur	Trachypithecus obscurus					x				x		NT
Phayre's Langur	Trachypithecus phayrei				x	x				x	x	EN
Capped Langur	Trachypithecus pileatus					x						VU
Cat Ba Langur	Trachypithecus poliocephalus										x	CR
Shortridge's Langur	Trachypithecus shortridgei					x						EN
Hominidae												
Sumatran Orangutan	Pongo abelii			x								CR
Bornean Orangutan	Pongo pygmaeus			x			x					EN
Hylobatidae												
Hoolock	Hoolock hoolock					x						EN
Agile Gibbon	Hylobates agilis			x			x			x		EN
Bornean White-bearded Gibbon	Hylobates albibarbis			x								EN
Kloss's Gibbon	Hylobates klossii			x								EN

English name	Scientific name	BN	KH	ID	LA	MM	MY	PH	SG	TH	VN	IUCN
White-handed Gibbon	Hylobates lar			x	x	x	x			x		EN
Javan Gibbon	Hylobates moloch			x								EN
Müller's Bornean Gibbon	Hylobates muelleri	x		x			x					EN
Pileated Gibbon	Hylobates pileatus		x		x					x		EN
Black Crested Gibbon	Nomascus concolor				x						x	CR
Buff-cheeked Gibbon	Nomascus gabriellae		x		x						x	EN
Northern White-cheeked Gibbon	Nomascus leucogenys				x						x	CR
Cao-Vit Crested Gibbon	Nomascus nasutus										x	CR
Southern White-cheeked Gibbon	Nomascus siki				x		x				x	EN
Siamang	Symphalangus syndactylus			x			x			x		EN
Lorisidae												
Northern Slow Loris	Nycticebus bengalensis		x		x	x	x			x	x	VU
Sunda Slow Loris	Nycticebus coucang			x			x		x	x		VU
Javan Slow Loris	Nycticebus javanicus			x								EN
Bornean Slow Loris	Nycticebus menagensis	x		x			x	x				VU
Pygmy Loris	Nycticebus pygmaeus		x		x		x				x	VU
Tarsiidae												
Western Tarsier	Tarsius bancanus	x		x			x					VU
Philippine Tarsier	Tarsius syrichta							x				NT
PROBOSCIDEA												
Elephantidae												
Asian Elephant	Elephas maximus		x	x	x	x	x			x	x	EN
RODENTIA												
Cricetidae												
Kachin Vole	Eothenomys cachinus					x				x	x	LC
Père David's Vole	Eothenomys melanogaster				x	x				x	x	LC

English name	Scientific name	BN	KH	ID	LA	MM	MY	PH	SG	TH	VN	IUCN
Clarke's Vole	Microtus clarkei					×						LC
Forrest's Mountain Vole	Neodon forresti					×						DD
Diatomyidae												
Kha-nyou	Laonastes aenigmamus				×							EN
Hystricidae												
Asian Brush-tailed Porcupine	Atherurus macrourus		×		×	×	×			×	×	LC
East Asian Porcupine	Hystrix brachyura	×	×	×	×	×	×		×	×	×	LC
Thick-spined Porcupine	Hystrix crassispinis	×		×			×					LC
Sunda Porcupine	Hystrix javanica			×								LC
Palawan Porcupine	Hystrix pumila							×				VU
Sumatran Porcupine	Hystrix sumatrae			×								LC
Long-tailed Porcupine	Trichys fasciculata	×		×			×					LC
Muridae												
Luzon Broad-toothed Rat	Abditomys latidens							×				DD
Mindoro Climbing Rat	Anonymomys mindorensis							×				DD
South China Wood Mouse	Apodemus draco				×							LC
Large-eared Wood Mouse	Apodemus latronum				×							LC
Luzon Cordillera Forest Mouse	Apomys abrae							×				DD
Camiguin Forest Mouse	Apomys camiguenensis							×				VU
Luzon Montane Forest Mouse	Apomys datae							×				LC
Large Mindoro Forest Mouse	Apomys gracilirostris							×				DD
Mindanao Mossy Forest Mouse	Apomys hylocoetes							×				LC
Mindanao Montane Forest Mouse	Apomys insignis							×				LC
Mindanao Lowland Forest Mouse	Apomys littoralis							×				DD
Small Luzon Forest Mouse	Apomys microdon							×				LC
Least Philippine Forest Mouse	Apomys musculus							×				LC
Long-nosed Luzon Forest Mouse	Apomys sacobianus							×				DD

English name	Scientific name	BN	KH	ID	LA	MM	MY	PH	SG	TH	VN	IUCN
Cordillera Shrew Mouse	*Archboldomys kalinga*							×				LC
Isarog Shrew Mouse	*Archboldomys luzonensis*							×				VU
Palanan Shrew Mouse	*Archboldomys musseri*							×				LC
Lesser Bandicoot Rat	*Bandicota bengalensis*					×						LC
Greater Bandicoot Rat	*Bandicota indica*		×		×	×				×	×	LC
Savile's Bandicoot Rat	*Bandicota savilei*		×			×				×	×	LC
Large-toothed Hairy-tailed Rat	*Batomys dentatus*							×				DD
Luzon Hairy-tailed Rat	*Batomys granti*							×				NT
Dinagat Hairy-tailed Rat	*Batomys russatus*							×				EN
Hamiguitan Hairy-tailed Rat	*Batomys hamiguitan*							×				NE
Mindanao Hairy-tailed Rat	*Batomys salomonseni*							×				LC
Berdmore's Rat	*Berylmys berdmorei*		×		×	×				×	×	LC
Bowers's Rat	*Berylmys bowersi*			×	×	×	×			×	×	LC
Mackenzie's Rat	*Berylmys mackenziei*					×					×	DD
Manipur Rat	*Berylmys manipulus*					×						DD
Large Mindanao Forest Rat	*Bullimus bagobus*							×				LC
Camiguin Forest Rat	*Bullimus gamay*							×				VU
Large Luzon Forest Rat	*Bullimus luzonicus*							×				LC
Short-footed Luzon Tree Rat	*Carpomys melanurus*							×				DD
White-bellied Luzon Tree Rat	*Carpomys phaeurus*							×				LC
Fea's Tree Rat	*Chiromyscus chiropus*				×	×				×		LC
Palawan Pencil-tailed Tree Mouse	*Chiropodomys calamianensis*							×				DD
Indomalayan Pencil-tailed Tree Mouse	*Chiropodomys gliroides*		×	×	×	×	×			×	×	LC
Koopman's Pencil-tailed Tree Mouse	*Chiropodomys karlkoopmani*			×								EN
Large Pencil-tailed Tree Mouse	*Chiropodomys major*						×					DD
Grey-bellied Pencil-tailed Tree Mouse	*Chiropodomys muroides*			×			×					DD

English name	Scientific name	BN	KH	ID	LA	MM	MY	PH	SG	TH	VN	IUCN
Small Pencil-tailed Tree Mouse	Chiropodomys pusillus			x								DD
Isarog Striped Shrew Rat	Chrotomys gonzalesi							x				NT
Lowland Striped Shrew Rat	Chrotomys mindorensis							x				NT
Sibuyan Striped Shrew Rat	Chrotomys sibuyanensis							x				DD
Blazed Luzon Shrew Rat	Chrotomys silaceus							x				LC
Luzon Montane Striped Shrew Rat	Chrotomys whiteheadi							x				LC
Dinagat Hairy-tailed Cloud Rat	Crateromys australis							x				CR
Panay Bushy-tailed Cloud Rat	Crateromys heaneyi							x				EN
Ilin Hairy-tailed Cloud Rat	Crateromys paulus							x				DD
Luzon Bushy-tailed Cloud Rat	Crateromys schadenbergi							x				EN
Northern Luzon Shrew Mouse	Crunomys fallax							x				DD
Southern Philippine Shrew Mouse	Crunomys melanius							x				VU
Kitanglad Shrew Mouse	Crunomys suncoides							x				DD
Millard's Giant Rat	Dacnomys millardi				x							DD
Crump's Soft-furred Rat	Diomys crumpi					x						DD
Greater Ranee Mouse	Haeromys margarettae						x					DD
Lesser Ranee Mouse	Haeromys pusillus			x			x					DD
Lesser Marmoset Rat	Hapalomys delacouri				x			x				VU
Greater Marmoset Rat	Hapalomys longicaudatus					x	x			x	x	EN
Javan Bamboo Rat	Kadarsanomys sodyi			x								VU
Grey Tree Rat	Lenothrix canus						x					LC
Sundaic Mountain Rat	Leopoldamys ciliatus			x			x					LC
Edwards's Giant Rat	Leopoldamys edwardsi				x	x				x	x	LC
Miller's Giant Rat	Leopoldamys milleti										x	LC
Neill's Giant Rat	Leopoldamys neilli									x		DD
Long-tailed Giant Rat	Leopoldamys sabanus	x		x	x	x	x			x	x	LC
Mentawai Long-tailed Giant Rat	Leopoldamys siporanus			x								EN

English name	Scientific name	BN	KH	ID	LA	MM	MY	PH	SG	TH	VN	IUCN
Grey-bellied Moss Mouse	Limnomys bryophilus							x				LC
Long-tailed Moss Mouse	Limnomys sibuanus							x				LC
Mountain Maxomys	Maxomys alticola						x					LC
Small Maxomys	Maxomys baeodon						x					DD
Bartels's Javan Maxomys	Maxomys bartelsii			x								LC
Sumatran Mountain Maxomys	Maxomys hylomyoides			x								DD
Malayan Mountain Maxomys	Maxomys inas						x					LC
Broad-nosed Maxomys	Maxomys inflatus			x								VU
Indochinese Maxomys	Maxomys moi				x						x	LC
Ochraceous-bellied Bornean Maxomys	Maxomys ochraceiventer			x			x					DD
Mentawai Maxomys	Maxomys pagensis			x								EN
Palawan Maxomys	Maxomys panglima							x				LC
Rajah Maxomys	Maxomys rajah	x		x			x		x	x		VU
Red Spiny Maxomys	Maxomys surifer	x	x	x	x	x	x			x	x	LC
Whitehead's Maxomys	Maxomys whiteheadi	x		x			x			x		VU
Harvest Mouse	Micromys minutus					x					x	LC
Popa Soft-furred Rat	Millardia kathleenae					x						LC
Little Indian Field Mouse	Mus booduga					x						LC
Ricefield Mouse	Mus caroli		x		x	x	x			x	x	LC
Fawn-coloured Mouse	Mus cervicolor		x		x	x				x	x	LC
Cook's Mouse	Mus cookii				x	x				x	x	LC
Sumatran Shrewlike Mouse	Mus crociduroides			x								DD
Sheath-tailed Mouse	Mus fragilicauda				x					x		DD
Indochinese Shrewlike Mouse	Mus pahari		x		x	x				x	x	LC
Shortridge's Mouse	Mus shortridgei		x		x	x				x	x	LC
Volcano Mouse	Mus vulcani			x								VU

English name	Scientific name	BN	KH	ID	LA	MM	MY	PH	SG	TH	VN	IUCN
Banahaw Tree Mouse	Musseromys gulantang							×				NE
Brahman Niviventer	Niviventer brahma					×						LC
Cameron Highlands Niviventer	Niviventer cameroni						×					VU
Confucian Niviventer	Niviventer confucianus					×				×	×	LC
Dark-tailed Niviventer	Niviventer cremoriventer			×			×			×		VU
Smoke-bellied Niviventer	Niviventer eha					×						LC
Montane Sumatran Niviventer	Niviventer fraternus			×								LC
Indomalayan Niviventer	Niviventer fulvescens		×	×	×	×	×			×	×	LC
Limestone Niviventer	Niviventer hinpoon									×		DD
Indochinese Arboreal Niviventer	Niviventer langbianis		×		×	×				×	×	LC
Montane Javan Niviventer	Niviventer lepturus			×								LC
Montane Bornean Niviventer	Niviventer rapit			×			×					LC
Indochinese Mountain Niviventer	Niviventer tenaster		×		×	×				×	×	LC
Palawan Mountain Rat	Palawanomys furvus							×				DD
Southern Luzon Giant Cloud Rat	Phloeomys cumingi							×				VU
Northern Luzon Giant Cloud Rat	Phloeomys pallidus							×				LC
Red Tree Rat	Pithecheir melanurus			×								VU
Malayan Tree Rat	Pithecheir parvus						×					DD
Sunburned Rat	Rattus adustus			×								DD
Indochinese Forest Rat	Rattus andamanensis		×		×	×				×	×	LC
Annandale's Rat	Rattus annandalei			×			×		×			LC
Ricefield Rat	Rattus argentiventer		×	×	×		×	×		×	×	LC
Kinabalu Rat	Rattus baluensis						×					LC
Aceh Rat	Rattus blangorum			×								DD
Enggano Island Rat	Rattus enganus			×								DD
Philippine Forest Rat	Rattus everetti							×				LC
Pacific Rat	Rattus exulans	×	×	×	×	×	×	×	×	×	×	LC

English name	Scientific name	BN	KH	ID	LA	MM	MY	PH	SG	TH	VN	IUCN
Hoogerwerf's Rat	*Rattus hoogerwerfi*			×								VU
Sumatran Mountain Rat	*Rattus korinchi*			×								DD
Lesser Ricefield Rat	*Rattus losea*		×		×					×	×	LC
Mentawai Rat	*Rattus lugens*			×								EN
Mindoro Mountain Rat	*Rattus mindorensis*							×				DD
White-footed Indochinese Rat	*Rattus nitidus*				×	×				×	×	LC
Osgood's Rat	*Rattus osgoodi*										×	LC
Simalur Rat	*Rattus simalurensis*			×								EN
Tanezumi Rat	*Rattus tanezumi*		×		×		×	×	×	×	×	LC
Tawi-tawi Forest Rat	*Rattus tawitawiensis*							×				DD
Malaysian Wood Rat	*Rattus tiomanicus*	×		×			×	×	×	×		LC
Banahao Shrew Rat	*Rhynchomys banahao*							×				DD
Isarog Shrew Rat	*Rhynchomys isarogensis*							×				VU
Northern Luzon Shrew Rat	*Rhynchomys soricoides*							×				NT
Zambales Shrew Rat	*Rhynchomys tapulao*							×				DD
Lao Limestone Rat	*Saxatilomys paulinae*				×							DD
Mountain Giant Rat	*Sundamys infraluteus*			×			×					LC
Bartels's Rat	*Sundamys maxi*			×								EN
Müller's Rat	*Sundamys muelleri*	×		×		×	×	×		×		LC
Mindanao Dusky Rat	*Tarsomys apoensis*							×				LC
Mindanao Spiny Rat	*Tarsomys echinatus*							×				VU
Tonkin Limestone Rat	*Tonkinomys daovantieni*										×	DD
Luzon Short-nosed Rat	*Tryphomys adustus*							×				DD
Long-tailed Climbing Mouse	*Vandeleuria oleracea*		×			×				×	×	LC
Vernay's Climbing Mouse	*Vernaya fulva*					×						LC
Platacanthomyidae												
Soft-furred Pygmy-dormouse	*Typhlomys cinereus*										×	LC

English name	Scientific name	BN	KH	ID	LA	MM	MY	PH	SG	TH	VN	IUCN
Sciuridae												
Black Flying Squirrel	*Aeromys tephromelas*	×		×			×			×		DD
Thomas's Flying Squirrel	*Aeromys thomasi*	×		×			×					DD
Hairy-footed Flying Squirrel	*Belomys pearsonii*				×	×				×	×	DD
Ear-spot Squirrel	*Callosciurus adamsi*						×					VU
Kloss's Squirrel	*Callosciurus albescens*			×								DD
Kinabalu Squirrel	*Callosciurus baluensis*						×					LC
Grey-bellied Squirrel	*Callosciurus caniceps*				×	×	×			×		LC
Pallas's Squirrel	*Callosciurus erythraeus*		×		×	×	×			×	×	LC
Variable Squirrel	*Callosciurus finlaysonii*		×		×	×				×	×	LC
Inornate Squirrel	*Callosciurus inornatus*				×						×	LC
Mentawai Squirrel	*Callosciurus melanogaster*			×								VU
Sunda Black-banded Squirrel	*Callosciurus nigrovittatus*			×			×			×		NT
Plantain Squirrel	*Callosciurus notatus*	×		×			×		×	×		LC
Bornean Black-banded Squirrel	*Callosciurus orestes*			×			×					LC
Phayre's Squirrel	*Callosciurus phayrei*					×						LC
Prevost's Squirrel	*Callosciurus prevostii*	×		×			×			×		LC
Irrawaddy Squirrel	*Callosciurus pygerythrus*					×						LC
Stripe-bellied Squirrel	*Callosciurus quinquestriatus*					×						NT
Bornean Mountain Ground Squirrel	*Dremomys everetti*			×			×					LC
Red-throated Squirrel	*Dremomys gularis*										×	LC
Orange-bellied Squirrel	*Dremomys lokriah*					×						LC
Perny's Long-nosed Squirrel	*Dremomys pernyi*					×						LC
Red-hipped Squirrel	*Dremomys pyrrhomerus*										×	LC
Red-cheeked Squirrel	*Dremomys rufigenis*		×		×	×	×			×	×	LC
Philippine Pygmy Squirrel	*Exilisciurus concinnus*							×				LC
Plain Pygmy Squirrel	*Exilisciurus exilis*	×		×			×					DD

English name	Scientific name	BN	KH	ID	LA	MM	MY	PH	SG	TH	VN	IUCN
Tufted Pygmy Squirrel	Exilisciurus whiteheadi	×		×			×					LC
Sculptor Squirrel	Glyphotes simus						×					DD
Particoloured Flying Squirrel	Hylopetes alboniger		×		×	×				×	×	LC
Bartels's Flying Squirrel	Hylopetes bartelsi			×								DD
Grey-cheeked Flying Squirrel	Hylopetes lepidus			×			×					DD
Palawan Flying Squirrel	Hylopetes nigripes							×				NT
Phayre's Flying Squirrel	Hylopetes phayrei				×	×				×	×	LC
Jentink's Flying Squirrel	Hylopetes platyurus			×			×			×		DD
Sipora Flying Squirrel	Hylopetes sipora			×								EN
Red-cheeked Flying Squirrel	Hylopetes spadiceus	×	×	×	×	×	×		×	×	×	LC
Sumatran Flying Squirrel	Hylopetes winstoni			×								DD
Horsfield's Flying Squirrel	Iomys horsfieldii	×		×			×		×			LC
Mentawai Flying Squirrel	Iomys sipora			×								EN
Four-striped Ground Squirrel	Lariscus hosei			×			×					NT
Three-striped Ground Squirrel	Lariscus insignis	×		×			×			×		LC
Niobe Ground Squirrel	Lariscus niobe			×								DD
Mentawai Ground Squirrel	Lariscus obscurus			×								NT
Berdmore's Ground Squirrel	Menetes berdmorei		×		×	×				×	×	LC
Black-eared Pygmy Squirrel	Nannosciurus melanotis	×		×			×					LC
Lesser Pygmy Flying Squirrel	Petaurillus emiliae						×					DD
Hose's Pygmy Flying Squirrel	Petaurillus hosei	×					×					DD
Selangor Pygmy Flying Squirrel	Petaurillus kinlochii						×					DD
Spotted Giant Flying Squirrel	Petaurista elegans			×	×	×	×			×	×	LC
Red Giant Flying Squirrel	Petaurista petaurista	×		×	×	×	×			×		LC
Indian Giant Flying Squirrel	Petaurista philippensis		×		×	×				×	×	LC
Mindanao Flying Squirrel	Petinomys crinitus							×				LC
Whiskered Flying Squirrel	Petinomys genibarbis	×		×			×					VU

English name	Scientific name	BN	KH	ID	LA	MM	MY	PH	SG	TH	VN	IUCN
Hagen's Flying Squirrel	*Petinomys hageni*			x								DD
Siberut Flying Squirrel	*Petinomys lugens*			x								EN
Arrow Flying Squirrel	*Petinomys sagitta*			x								DD
Temminck's Flying Squirrel	*Petinomys setosus*	x		x		x	x			x		VU
Vordermann's Flying Squirrel	*Petinomys vordermanni*	x		x		x	x			x		VU
Smoky Flying Squirrel	*Pteromyscus pulverulentus*	x		x			x			x		EN
Cream-coloured Giant Squirrel	*Ratufa affinis*	x		x			x			x		NT
Black Giant Squirrel	*Ratufa bicolor*		x	x	x	x	x		x	x	x	NT
Tufted Ground Squirrel	*Rheithrosciurus macrotis*	x		x			x					VU
Shrew-faced Ground Squirrel	*Rhinosciurus laticaudatus*	x		x			x		x	x		NT
Brooke's Squirrel	*Sundasciurus brookei*											LC
Davao Squirrel	*Sundasciurus davensis*							x				DD
Fraternal Squirrel	*Sundasciurus fraterculus*			x								EN
Horse-tailed Squirrel	*Sundasciurus hippurus*	x		x			x			x		NT
Busuanga Squirrel	*Sundasciurus hoogstraali*							x				LC
Jentink's Squirrel	*Sundasciurus jentinki*						x					LC
Northern Palawan Squirrel	*Sundasciurus juvencus*							x				LC
Low's Squirrel	*Sundasciurus lowii*	x		x			x					LC
Mindanao Squirrel	*Sundasciurus mindanensis*							x				LC
Culion Squirrel	*Sundasciurus moellendorffi*							x				NT
Philippine Squirrel	*Sundasciurus philippinensis*							x				LC
Palawan Montane Squirrel	*Sundasciurus rabori*							x				DD
Samar Squirrel	*Sundasciurus samarensis*							x				LC
Southern Palawan Montane Squirrel	*Sundasciurus steerii*							x				LC
Slender Squirrel	*Suncasciurus tenuis*	x		x			x		x	x		LC
Western Striped Squirrel	*Tamiops mcclellandii*		x		x	x	x			x	x	LC
Eastern Striped Squirrel	*Tamiops maritimus*				x						x	LC

169

English name	Scientific name	BN	KH	ID	LA	MM	MY	PH	SG	TH	VN	IUCN
Cambodian Striped Squirrel	*Tamiops rodolphii*		×		×					×	×	LC
Swinhoe's Striped Squirrel	*Tamiops swinhoei*					×					×	LC
Spalacidae												
Lesser Bamboo Rat	*Cannomys badius*		×		×	×				×	×	LC
Hoary Bamboo Rat	*Rhizomys pruinosus*		×		×	×	×			×	×	LC
Chinese Bamboo Rat	*Rhizomys sinensis*					×					×	LC
Indomalayan Bamboo Rat	*Rhizomys sumatrensis*		×	×	×	×	×			×	×	LC
SCANDENTIA												
Ptilocercidae												
Feather-tailed Treeshrew	*Ptilocercus lowii*	×		×			×			×		LC
Tupaiidae												
Bornean Slender-tailed Treeshrew	*Dendrogale melanura*	×		×			×					DD
Northern Slender-tailed Treeshrew	*Dendrogale murina*		×		×						×	LC
Northern Treeshrew	*Tupaia belangeri*		×		×	×	×			×	×	LC
Golden-bellied Treeshrew	*Tupaia chrysogaster*			×								EN
Striped Treeshrew	*Tupaia dorsalis*	×		×			×					DD
Common Treeshrew	*Tupaia glis*			×			×		×	×		LC
Slender Treeshrew	*Tupaia gracilis*	×		×			×					LC
Horsfield's Treeshrew	*Tupaia javanica*			×								LC
Bornean Treeshrew	*Tupaia longipes*	×		×			×					LC
Lesser Treeshrew	*Tupaia minor*	×		×			×			×		LC
Mountain Treeshrew	*Tupaia montana*	×		×			×					LC
Palawan Treeshrew	*Tupaia palawanensis*							×				LC
Painted Treeshrew	*Tupaia picta*	×		×			×					LC
Ruddy Treeshrew	*Tupaia splendidula*			×								LC
Large Treeshrew	*Tupaia tana*	×		×			×					LC
Mindanao Treeshrew	*Urogale everetti*							×				LC

MARINE MAMMALS

English name	Scientific name	IUCN
CETACEA		
Balaenopteridae		
Minke Whale	*Balaenoptera acutorostrata*	LC
Sei Whale	*Balaenoptera borealis*	EN
Bryde's Whale	*Balaenoptera edeni*	DD
Blue Whale	*Balaenoptera musculus*	EN
Omura's Whale	*Balaenoptera omurai*	DD
Fin Whale	*Balaenoptera physalus*	EN
Humpback Whale	*Megaptera novaeangliae*	LC
Delphinidae		
Long-beaked Common Dolphin	*Delphinus capensis*	DD
Pygmy Killer Whale	*Feresa attenuata*	DD
Short-finned Pilot Whale	*Globicephala macrorhynchus*	DD
Risso's Dolphin	*Grampus griseus*	LC
Fraser's Dolphin	*Lagenodelphis hosei*	LC
Irrawaddy Dolphin	*Orcaella brevirostris*	VU
Killer Whale	*Orcinus orca*	DD
Melon-headed Whale	*Peponocephala electra*	LC
False Killer Whale	*Pseudorca crassidens*	DD
Indo-Pacific Humpbacked Dolphin	*Sousa chinensis*	NT
Pantropical Spotted Dolphin	*Stenella attenuata*	LC
Striped Dolphin	*Stenella coeruleoalba*	LC
Spinner Dolphin	*Stenella longirostris*	DD
Rough-toothed Dolphin	*Steno bredanensis*	LC
Indo-Pacific Bottlenose Dolphin	*Tursiops aduncus*	DD
Common Bottlenose Dolphin	*Tursiops truncatus*	LC
Phocoenidae		
Indo-pacific Finless Porpoise	*Neophocaena phocaenoides*	VU
Physeteridae		
Pygmy Sperm Whale	*Kogia breviceps*	DD
Dwarf Sperm Whale	*Kogia sima*	DD
Great Sperm Whale	*Physeter macrocephalus*	VU
Ziphiidae		
Longman's Beaked Whale	*Indopacetus pacificus*	DD
Blainville's Beaked Whale	*Mesoplodon densirostris*	DD
Ginkgo-toothed Beaked Whale	*Mesoplodon ginkgodens*	DD
Cuvier's Beaked Whale	*Ziphius cavirostris*	LC
SIRENIA		
Dugongidae		
Dugong	*Dugong dugon*	VU

▪ Further Information and References ▪

Further information

A number of books and online resources have been extremely useful in the development of this book. Additionally, there are numerous peer-reviewed publications that are highly informative, such as Duckworth and Pine's 'English names for a world list of mammals, exemplified by species of Indochina' (*Mammal Review*, 2003, Vol. 33, 151–173), which guided the further improvement and standardisation of common English names for South-East Asian mammals. We recommend the following, but there are also many other useful resources that are not listed here. Also included are the specialist groups, which are networks of experts in the respective species groups, under the umbrella of the IUCN's Species Survival Commission.

References and further reading

Baker, N. and Lim, K. (2008). *Wild Animals of Singapore: a Photographic Guide to Mammals, Reptiles, Amphibians and Freshwater Fish.* Draco Publishing & Distribution and Nature Society Singapore, Singapore.

Carwardine, M. (2006). *Whales, Dolphins and Porpoises.* HarperCollins, London, UK.

Ecology Asia (2012). www.ecologyasia.com. Singapore.

Francis, C. M. (2001). *A Photographic Guide to the Mammals of South-East Asia.* New Holland, London, UK.

Francis, C. M. (2008). *A Field Guide to the Mammals of South-East Asia.* New Holland, London, UK.

Groves, C. and Grubb, P. (2011). *Ungulate Taxonomy.* Johns Hopkins University Press, Baltimore, MD, USA.

IUCN (2012). *The IUCN Red List of Threatened Species. Version 2012.1.* www.iucnredlist.org.

Lekagul, B. and McNeely, L. (1977). *Mammals of Thailand.* Association for the Conservation of Wildlife, Bangkok, Thailand.

Lim, N. (2007). *Colugo: the Flying Lemur of South-east Asia.* Draco Publishing & Distribution and the National University of Singapore, Singapore.

Kingston, T., Lim, B. L. and Zubaid, A. (2006). *Bats of Krau Wildlife Reserve.* Penerbit Universiti Kebangsaan Malaysia, Bangi, Malaysia.

Krëb, D. (2004). *Facultative river dolphins: conservation and social ecology of freshwater and coastal Irrawaddy Dolphins in Indonesia.* Institute for Biodiversity and Ecosystem Dynamics / Zoologisch Museum Amsterdam.

Kruuk, H. (2006). *Otters: Ecology, Behavior and Conservation.* Oxford University Press, New York, NY, USA.

Parr, W. K. J. and Hoang Xuan Thuy (2008). *A Field Guide to the Large Mammals of Vietnam.* People and Nature Reconciliation (PanNature). Thong Tan Publishing House, Hanoi, Vietnam.

Payne, J., Francis, C. M. and Phillipps, K. (1985). *A Field Guide to the Mammals of Borneo.* The Sabah Society, Malaysia.

Redmond, I. (2008). *Primates of the World.* New Holland, London, UK.

Smith, A. T. and Xie, Y. (2008). *Mammals of China.* Princeton University Press, Princeton, NJ, USA.

Synopsis of Philippine Mammals (2012). archive.fieldmuseum.org/philippine_mammals.

Relevant IUCN SSC specialist groups

Asian Elephant Specialist Group – www.asesg.org
Asian Rhino Specialist Group – www.rhinos.org/professional-resources/iucn-asian-rhino-specialist
Asian Wild Cattle Specialist Group – www.asianwildcattle.org
Bat Specialist Group – www.iucnbsg.org
Bear Specialist Group – www.bearbiology.com
Canid Specialist Group – www.canids.org
Caprinae Specialist Group – pages.usherbrooke.ca/mfesta/iucnwork.htm
Cat Specialist Group – www.catsg.org
Cetacean Specialist Group – www.iucn-csg.org
Deer Specialist Group – www.iibce.edu.uy/DEER/english.htm
Lagomorph Specialist Group – www.iucn.org/about/work/programmes/species/who_we_are/ssc_
    specialist_groups_and_red_list_authorities_directory/mammals/lagomorph_specialist_group
Otter Specialist Group – www.otterspecialistgroup.org
Pangolin Specialist Group (www.pangolinsg.org)
Primate Specialist Group – www.primate-sg.org
Sirenia Specialist Group – www.locus-nq.net/iucnssg
Small Carnivore Specialist Group – www.smallcarnivoreconservation.org/scc/Small_Carnivore_
    Specialist_Group
Small Mammal Specialist Group (no website)
Tapir Specialist Group – www.tapirs.org
Wild Pig Specialist Group – data.iucn.org/themes/ssc/sgs/pphsg/home.htm

Acknowledgements

This book would not have been possible without input and support from many individuals working on mammal conservation in South-East Asia, and the very generous contributions of photographs from these same individuals, as well as others.

All photographers are credited on page 176. However, we would especially like to thank the following for helping track down hard-to-come-by photos, for providing information and for being very supportive of this project. We are fortunate to call them friends. Thanks to Abraham Mathew, Barney Long, Celine Low, Danielle Krëb, Jasmine Steed, James Eaton, Matt Linkie, Matt Struebig, Neil Furey, Nick Baker, Pilar Salajeno, Resit Sozer, Sabine Schoppe and Serge Wich. We extend a special thanks to Will Duckworth for providing extremely useful information and advice, for reviewing earlier drafts, and for tirelessly responding to countless questions!

We would also like to thank John Beaufoy, Ken Scriven, Rosemary Wilkinson, Hugh Brazier and David Price-Goodfellow for pulling the whole project together.

A note of mention to the researchers and conservation workers, who tirelessly toil in the field to better understand and protect the mammals of South-East Asia.

About the authors

Dr Chris R. Shepherd and Loretta Ann Shepherd are a husband-and-wife team based in Malaysia, working on wildlife conservation issues throughout South-East Asia. Both strongly believe that an increased appreciation for wildlife is key to conservation success.

▪ INDEX ▪

Photo credits

Photos are denoted by a page number followed where relevant by t (top), b (bottom), l (left) or r (right.)

Nick Baker, EcologyAsia.com: 16, 17l, 17r, 20l, 20r, 21, 22l, 22r, 26, 29, 61, 89, 118, 119, 121, 123, 124l, 124r, 133, 134, 135. Elizabeth A. Burgess: 93l, 93r. Dan Challender/Carnivore and Pangolin Conservation Program, Vietnam: 12l. Iing Cikananga: 42r, 100l, 100r. Leanne Clark/ Carnivore and Pangolin Conservation Program, Vietnam: 13. Roger G. Dolorosa/Western Philippines University: 104, 138. Vilma D'Rozario/Cicada Tree Eco-Place: 70, 86. Duc Hoang Minh: 46. Nicole Duplaix: 64, 65l, 65r, 66. James Eaton/Birdtour Asia: 12r, 34, 43, 44l, 44r, 54, 55t, 69, 75, 94, 108, 126, 129l, 129r, 131. Fletcher & Baylis: 25, 56, 68, 106, 107l, 107r, 111, 136l, 136r, 137. Gabriella Fredriksson: 38, 39. Neil Furey: 23, 24, 27, 28. Melvin Gumal/ Wildlife Conservation Society Malaysia Program 19. Stephen Hogg/Wildtrack Photography: 4, 7, 14b, 51, 52t, 52b, 55bl, 55br, 80l, 80r, 95t, 95b, 97l, 97r. Kadoorie Farm & Botanic Garden, Hong Kong: 78. Kae Kawanishi/MYCAT: 77, 81, 84, 96, 99, 115. Kimabajo: 15, 58r, 101, 103, 105l. Danielle Krëb/Conservation Foundation for Rare Aquatic Species of Indonesia: 88, 90, 91, 92. Ch'ien C. Lee/Carnivore and Pangolin Conservation Program, Vietnam: 73. Celine Low: 36, 37, 76, 113, 125, 127, 128. Abraham Mathew: 112l, 112r. Abraham Mathew/ Singapore Zoo and Night Safari: 45, 57, 87l, 87r. Mohamed & Wilting, Sabah Wildlife Department, Sabah Forestry Department: 14t, 63, 74, 79t, 79b, 82, 83, 85. Richard Moore, International Animal Rescue: 30, 31, 33. NHPA/Gerald Cubitt: 72, 139. NHPA/Oscar Dominguez: 102. NHPA/Daniel Heuclin: 114. Pilar Saldajeno: 109r. Chris R. Shepherd: 9, 40, 41, 47, 48l, 48r, 49l, 49tr, 49br, 50l, 50r, 59, 71l, 71r, 105r, 120. John Steed: 122. Sabine Stolzenburg: 67. Ulrike Streicher: 32, 62. Magdalena Svensson: 42l. Rob Tizard: 18, 53. Jonah van Beijnen, Centre for Sustainability, Philippines: 130l, 130r. WCS Myanmar Program: 60b, 60t, 110, 116. Serge Wich: 35. Peter Widmann: 109l, 132. Wong Siew Te/Bornean Sun Bear Conservation Centre: 58l. WWF/CTNPCP/Mike Baltzer: 98. WWF/Toon Fey: 117.